Edited by John Foster

MACMILLAN ENGLISH

Newspapers

JOHN PRICE

MACMILLAN

First published 1991

Published by
MACMILLAN EDUCATION LTD
Houndmills, Basingstoke, Hampshire RG21 2XS
and London
Companies and representatives
throughout the world

Printed in Hong Kong

British Library Cataloguing in Publication Data
Price, John
Newspapers.–(Macmillan English)
1. Newspapers. Production
I. Title
070.172

ISBN 0–333–52231–1

ACKNOWLEDGEMENTS

The author and publishers wish to thank the following who have kindly given permission for the use of copyright material.

Action Holidays for advertising material; AC Press Services on behalf of the artist for cartoons by Charles Griffin; City Limits Publications for the review, 'The British are Coming' by Stephen Dinsdale, *City Limits*, 7th Dec. 1989; Early Times for material from various issues of *Early Times*; Express Newspapers plc for material from various editions of the *Daily Express* and *Daily Star*; The Independent for material from various issues of *The Independent*; The Indy for extracts from publicity material and various issues of *The Indy*; Livewire UK for an extract from their publicity material; Caroline Penn for the photograph included in the Save the Children advertisement; Save the Children for advertising material; Scoop for material from various issues of *Scoop*; Solo Syndication & Literary Agency Ltd for 'Dodging lessons at the Hi-de-hi school', *Daily Mail*, 6th Nov 1987; Miriam Stoppard for material included in the *Sunderland Echo*, 25th May 1988; Sunderland & Hartlepool Publishing and Printing Ltd for material from two issues of the *Sunderland Echo*; Syndication International Ltd for material from various issues of the *Daily Mirror*; Today for material from various issues of *Today*.

We are grateful to the following for permission to reproduce photographs: Associated Press, Camera Press, The Guardian, South West News, Sunderland Echo and Syndication International.

Every effort has been made to trace all copyright holders, but if any have been inadvertently overlooked the publishers will be pleased to make the necessary arrangement at the first opportunity.

Editorial coordination by
Gill Stacey and Liz Paren
Text design by Susan Clarke
Cover design by Quadraphic
Illustrations by Taurus Graphics

CONTENTS

INTRODUCTION

The Newspaper module in the *Macmillan English* series is a flexible resource of eleven assignments. Its central aim is to develop students' understanding of the various types and styles of communication to be found in newspapers and to provide them with opportunities to practise writing in many different forms, ranging from reports and feature articles to editorials and reviews.

The assignments and suggested tasks are directly related to the National Curriculum attainment targets and programmes of study for Key Stage 3, which stress the importance of developing the student's ability to read and understand non-literary materials and to write for a wide range of purposes and audiences. The study of newspapers also has a significant part to play in the development of students' knowledge about language for it includes, as do all the aspects of media education, dealing with 'fundamental questions of language interpretation and meaning' (*English 5–16* para 14.4).

The assignments cover a wide range of types of communication – reporting, persuading, describing, explaining, reviewing, satirising and expressing points of view – and include materials from newspapers for young people, such as *The Indy* and *Early Times* as well as from the popular and 'quality' daily papers. There are also sections on cartoons, graphics and photographs, for, as *English 5–16* says, students should be taught 'that pictures and other visual media can also convey meaning'. The tasks invite students to explore and analyse the different types of writing through pair and group discussion activities. The tasks also provide opportunities for them to practise the techniques they have observed by writing pieces which can be put together to make a group newspaper in the final assignment.

The module thus provides a wealth of opportunities for collaborative work in both speaking and listening, and writing. The assignments and tasks encourage a holistic approach to reading, speaking and listening, and writing. A consequence of this is that the possible language outcomes are enormous and the tasks are likely to generate responses across the entire Key Stage 3 range of attainment levels from 3 to 8. This should not be seen as a problem, but as an opportunity to guide and develop achievement to the maximum.

In relation to assessment it is important that the statements and levels of attainment set out in the statutory orders inform rather than overwhelm judgement and good practice.

For such a complex act as reading there can be no easy relationship between the processes of responding and making meaning and a figure on a ten point scale. The gradual growth of reading sophistication cannot be characterised as the simple acquisition of additional skills, whilst moving on a linear track. The processes of speaking and listening and of writing are similarly complex and equally difficult to plot on a scale. In both cases, the level of sophistication a student achieves will vary according to the task and its context.

Assessment needs, therefore, to be made over an extended period of time, during which the teacher builds up a picture of the student's performance, rather than by compiling a checklist after the completion of each task. Further suggestions for recording and assessment are made on Sheets 72–73.

It is useful to clarify the criteria used to link the assignments and tasks to the detailed requirements of the statements of attainment:

The assignments and tasks suggested here enable students to

1 *Develop the skills of speaking and listening* by giving opportunities to
- express points of view about topical issues
- engage in small group discussions of peer group work
- present arguments in a semi-formal environment
- organise and produce a newspaper for a real audience after reaching a consensus
- express judgements about news values and relevance
- interview people in order to find stories

2 *Develop writing in a range of forms* by giving opportunities to
- write reports, letters, reviews, cartoons, editorials and summaries
- structure stories and features
- re-draft
- write for different, real audiences
- take notes and re-write them
- devise appropriate headlines
- write succinctly and meet deadlines

3 *Develop the ability to read critically* by giving opportunities to
- study media texts
- detect bias
- understand the techniques of persuasive writing
- read for implied meanings
- make comparisons between texts
- look for evidence that supports opinions
- evaluate stories
- practise image analysis

4 *Improve presentational skills* by encouraging pupils to
- become aware of how newspapers are designed
- design layouts to help communication
- use word processors in the design of publications
- become more aware of how the concept of audience affects a publication

(For teachers who would welcome a sifting and sorting of those statements of attainment most directly addressed in this module, see Sheet 74.)

John Price

THE ASSIGNMENTS

Note: The symbol ✉ refers to the pieces of writing which students will keep for publishing their own newspaper when they have worked through the course.

ASSIGNMENT 1 **PLANNING YOUR OWN NEWSPAPER**

Aim To be aware of audience and the need to plan ahead

This activity gives specific direction and framework to the whole module by emphasising the need to write for a purpose and to identify the needs of the receivers of the writer's message. The first and last assignments are intended to give coherence and continuity to the rest of the module.

TASK 1 gives an example of a statement of intent which implies a clear knowledge of the needs of an audience.

TASK 2 encourages students to focus on the need to vary tone and style in addressing specific audiences.

Both tasks involve discussion which should lead to consensus and a small scale presentation for a peer group audience.
Suitable for attainment levels 4–8 in all three profile components.

While Task 3 is about presentation and layout and therefore directly related to attainment target 5, it is also related to developing the reading skills needed for level 7 and above.

ASSIGNMENT 2 **SHAPING NEWS STORIES**

Aim To be aware that writing can be carefully structured and to practise such writing

The talking, listening and writing are interwoven here as the students practise some simple journalistic techniques. The five Ws are meant to generate questions rather than to become a rigid formula. They are

invaluable to the insecure who find 'knowing what to write about' difficult, but they are only a starting point. You can make the interviews more challenging and realistic if you can use tape recorders or an internal telephone system.
Suitable for attainment levels 4–8 in all three profile components.

ASSIGNMENT 3 **WRITING TO THE POINT**

Aim To understand the techniques newspapers use to emphasise important information and to practise these techniques

The assignment moves the students on from thinking about structure and planning to thinking about style and clarity through brevity, which is one of the characteristics of good journalism.

Students have the opportunity to discuss meaning and style in small groups and to make judgements about what they read.

There is also the opportunity to think carefully about sound patterning in headline writing and there is encouragement of purposeful re-writing in the headline character exercise.

Students can also be encouraged to become aware of the typographical elements of style, such as the use of bold print and italics.
Suitable for attainment levels 4–8 in all profile components.

ASSIGNMENT 4 **WRITING ABOUT PEOPLE**

Aim To understand how journalists involve readers by writing about individual people with whom the reader can identify and to practise such techniques

There is more opportunity here for the changes that are made when transforming reported speech into direct speech and vice versa.

Task 4 is a demanding one and should not just be about mentioning people in a story. It is about focus. The writer is like a camera

classroom discussion and telephoning people outside the school.

The responses to Task 2 should provide opportunities to help students punctuate direct speech accurately and to understand moving from a long shot (general statement of the topic) to a close up (how an individual is affected by or relates to the topic).

Suitable for attainment levels 4–8 in all three profile components.

ASSIGNMENT 5 **FEATURE WRITING**

Aim To understand that newspapers contain more than just hard news and that a feature article is different from a news story

Students have the opportunity of practising some of the personalising skills acquired in Assignment 4 when they write their own features here. There is opportunity for some research in feature writing.

Students who have their own expertise in extra-curricular activities can be encouraged to use their knowledge to write specialist features.

Suitable for attainment levels 4–8 in all profile components.

ASSIGNMENT 6 **EXPRESSING OPINIONS**

Aim To understand how opinions are most effectively expressed in newspapers and to practise supporting opinion with evidence

The common thread in the tasks in this assignment is the need to be rational when arguing a particular point of view. Small

group discussion of the quality and the relevance of the reasoning supporting judgements is of crucial importance before students write their own opinions.

Suitable for attainment levels 5–8 in all three profile components.

ASSIGNMENT 7 **BIAS**

Aim To understand that most newspaper writing is subjective and that what you see depends on where you stand

The purpose of the assignment is to encourage students to read between lines and make inferences. The tasks here are

more demanding than in earlier assignments and some texts more complex. They ask the student to compare and evaluate reports of the same event from different points of view.

Suitable for attainment levels 4–8 in all three profile components.

ASSIGNMENT 8 USING PICTURES

Aim To understand how pictures convey meaning

In Task 1 the pictures provide material for basic work on single image analysis, which is best done in a speculative, open-ended discussion to begin with.

Students can be encouraged to make both news value judgements and aesthetic judgements about composition, angles, lighting and so on.

In Task 2 it is important to look closely at captions because they can be used so effectively to manipulate readers. We don't just believe what we see, we believe what we are told to see.

Follow-up work could involve students making collections of different newspaper representations of famous people. If they collect pictures of the Prime Minister, for example, they can begin to appreciate that the images presented will be very different in newspapers of different political persuasions.

Task 3 follow-up work could include a study of stereotyping. Students can collect cartoons from any source and study how, for instance, different occupations or youth sub-cultures, or old people are represented.

Task 4 aims to show pupils how complex information can be expressed succinctly and vividly in visual form.

In Task 5 the popular papers are shown to be particularly expert at breaking up text to make it more accessible. Students can compare different tabloids to see how effectively they use different type-styles; symbols to highlight items in lists; numbered lists of information (e.g. '20 things you didn't know about Freddie Starr's hamster'); crossheads (key words separating paragraphs as mini-headlines); different print sizes; tinted backgrounds or reverse print.

Suitable for attainment levels 4–8 in all three profile components. Task 5 focuses on reading and writing.

ASSIGNMENT 9 ADVERTISING

Aim To understand how persuasive techniques are used by advertisers

The display adverts here have been chosen because they are workmanlike and non-controversial, rather than because they are dramatic or influential. Much of newspaper advertising is of this pedestrian nature. This choice has been made so that students can concentrate on technique rather than on

moral or emotional aspects of advertising. Such work is probably better done with magazine and television advertising.

The classified adverts have been included as an example of how linguistic and financial economy can be linked.

Suitable for attainment levels 4–8 in all three profile components. Task 2 focuses on reading and writing.

ASSIGNMENT 10 THE PRESS RELEASE

Aim To be aware of the purpose and value of press releases

Many local newspapers will be willing to supply schools with redundant press releases. They provide excellent examples of

professional writing with a very specific purpose and are ideal for summarising and re-writing.

Suitable for attainment levels 4–6 in reading and writing.

ASSIGNMENT 11 PUBLISHING YOUR OWN NEWSPAPER

Aim To make judgements about the quality of work and its suitability for its intended audience and to print and distribute a newspaper

The editorial exercise is very important and enough time should be provided for it to be done carefully and rationally. Groups must be able to give clear reasons for their choices. The reasons can be concerned with: what audiences want to read; what they are able to read; what they have time to read; the need to cater for a variety of interests; the quality of the writing; the layout of pages; topicality; the need to encourage writers.

When the papers have been distributed, some market research can be done to see how the publication is received. Groups should evaluate their own as well as other groups' publications and should begin by praising what is good before suggesting improvements.

A chart *Newspaper in the curriculum*, on page 71, suggests ways in which this assignment can be linked to work in other subjects and developed as a cross-curricular activity.

Suitable for attainment levels 4–8 in all three profile components.

TASK
1

Audience

Aim To prepare a statement about your newspaper

Look at the extract from publicity about *The Indy* newspaper. It states clearly what kind of audience the paper is aimed at. Write a group report to describe

- *The Indy*'s target audience
- how the paper intends to appeal to its audience
- what you think of its aims.

 As you work through this module you will write different kinds of articles, and you can publish these as a real newspaper after the last assignment.

Before you begin the writing, you should have a clear idea of who you are writing for.

In small groups, with each group responsible for producing its own paper, decide who your publication is aimed at. Write a statement as a pre-launch notice like *The Indy*'s, where you state your aims and how you will try to please your audience.

▶ Audience

The Indy
Tel: 01-253-1222

A new national paper for the young & independent

We were wondering whether you'd be interested in covering the launch of our new paper, *The Indy*.

It's a lively, colourful, general-interest paper aimed at 13–15-year-olds.

Some people have said it is impossible to appeal to this whole age-group: they've said the group is too different from one end to the other.

We believe that there are some things *everybody* is interested in. And those are the stories we're going to run. *Great pictures, and interesting stories.*

This isn't a cut-down version of The Independent. We talk to our readers about things that directly (or indirectly) concern *them*.

We will be providing news digests (putting daily news stories in their larger context), features, science, arts, music, TV, video, fashion, beauty, letters, sports, and a series of really quite amazing competitions.

They range from the serious (readers will write a three minute film and David Puttnam will produce it), to the frivolous (win an hour's work on a demolition site wrecking ball).

We're arranging for our readers to win sessions in a flight simulator, coaching lessons from the Captain of England, a recording session with the best rock guitarist in the country. A national TV station is offering a day's work on the news crews to produce a story.

Tabloid newspapers used to provide a useful introduction to newspaper reading. The market has changed over the last decade and has left these papers either savagely political, or dangerously prurient—sometimes both.

We aim to provide a lively, *interesting* paper to both the press, and the world—*their* world—of current affairs.

Have a look at the promotion we're running up to the launch.

TASK

2 Finding a style

Aim To recognise the importance of a reporting style in communicating with the reader

Read the following versions of the same news story, and say which you think is the most sensational, and which the most restrained.

A

Haircut boy suspended

A 16-year-old boy has been suspended by his school because he had a skinhead haircut.

Headteacher, Colin Long, said that teenager Bill Walker has been sent home until his hair is longer.

Ironically, Bill's father was suspended from the same school for having long hair 19 years ago.

B

Hair we go!

Teenager Bill Walker was kicked out of school yesterday for having short hair.

Bill's extra close cut didn't go down too well with Colin Long, headmaster at his school in Liverpool: 'I told him to go home and come back when his hair has grown again. If he gets away with it, others will copy him.'

Bill's father wasn't too happy – he was suspended from the same school nineteen years ago – because his hair was too long!

C

Big boot for school skinhead

A teenage skinhead has been given the boot by his boss.

The rule-breaking rebel, William Walker, got his marching orders when his bare bonce made headmaster Colin Long's hair stand on end.

And tonsorial troublemaking runs in the family! Walker's dad was a long-haired hippy 19 years ago when he got the same kick up the pants at school.

In small groups, discuss any changes to the meaning of the story that the different styles produce. Does your attitude to the boy change, for instance?

Which version would you choose for your newspaper, and why?

3 Design a masthead

Aim To design a suitable masthead for your newspaper

On Sheet 5 are four mastheads from young people's newspapers.

In small groups discuss what *image* each paper is trying to give.
Look at the style and size of print, the logos and the slogans, if any,
and the choice of name.

 Design your own masthead and give a presentation to other
groups about the kind of image you are trying to establish.

If you are working with a word processor, try out different fonts until
you find the style that is best for your title. Some examples are
shown on the next sheet. Which do you think is the most successful?
Why?

▶ Design a masthead

Page design

Aim To practise planning page layouts

Newspaper pages do not just happen, they are designed. Study the three examples of page 6 of the *Daily Mirror*. Each one is from a different day's paper, but they are all set out in the same pattern.

In pairs, draw a master plan to show how the Sheet is designed. Use a grid like the one shown on page 10 to help you.

With your partner, note down the following and compare results in class:

- How many different *types* of article/information does the basic design accommodate?
- What is the proportion of pictures to text?
- What variations do you notice within the basic design? Look at each example page in turn.

▶ Page design

Now the Prince has an answer for his critics

GRIFFIN'S EYE

DRAGON DEVELOPMENTS
MILE UPON MILE OF FUNCTIONAL BUT BORING BUILDINGS

PRINCE CHARLES is furious about a new book written by a man he once trusted and publicly praised. Its author is the journalist Anthony Holden.

For years Charles has followed the advice given to fellow Royals by Queen Victoria: Never complain, never explain.

But such is his anger at what he considers the distortions and inaccuracies in Holden's biography that yesterday he set about putting the record straight.

The man he chose to speak out for him is Mr. Tom Shebbeare, director of the Prince's Trust, Charles's personal charity.

Mr. Shebbeare, who could only have acted with the personal approval of Charles himself, defends the Prince on several fronts.

● His alleged "frustrations" at being a Prince-in-waiting to succeed to the throne, without a "proper" job.
● His attitude to pop concerts and the stars who perform at them in aid of Charles's various charities.
● The so-called "dangers" of Charles interfering politically as he strives to help deprived people in the inner cities.

For the Prince, Holden's book — "pretty much fiction from beginning to end," says Mr Shebbeare — could scarely have been more ill-timed.

Leading

It comes at the very moment Charles is setting out to present a whole new image of himself as a leading European statesman.

The Prince feels betrayed by Holden. He considers the views and opinions in the biography are sensational and wildly inaccurate.

There was a time when the two men knew each other quite well. They attended the same dinner party at the British Ambassador's residence in Washington

Holden later gained the Prince's confidence sufficiently to win co-operation from Charles's personal staff on a book written at the time of the Prince's thirtieth birthday

But, says Charles, there has been no help since.

For the Prince, his trip to France with Princess

Life begins at 40 'New image as a Euro statesman'

by JAMES WHITAKER
Picture: KENT GAVIN

Diana last week was an important step in his ambition to be regarded as a statesman of significance

There is no question his visit was a total triumph, culminating as it did in his appearance at the side of President Mitterrand at the Arc de Triomphe on Armistice Day last Friday

It was an honour to the Prince and, in his position of heir to the British throne, without precedent. No foreigner has ever taken such an active role in the French remembrance service

This was not all Charles's tour of France was a State visit in all but name

He was received on arrival at the Elysee Palace by the President. He was accorded full honours on departure and he and Diana made an enormous impact on the French Prime Minister and other Cabinet Ministers, both on a personal and official level

The Prince has built up an imposing catalogue of achievements in recent years, not least through the Prince's Trust

The Trust has been particularly active in inner-city areas such as Halifax, Bradford and Birmingham where he will spend today, his birthday.

It has scored major successes, helping the young, the young unemployed, young offenders and even young life prisoners.

Says Mr Shebbeare "We have an astonishing success rate among people who have been turned down by normal finance projects."

"We would reckon a 5 per cent success rate would be good going, let alone 60 per cent which is what we have achieved"

Charles is NOT just a figurehead. He is deeply involved, attending numerous meetings, introducing influential people in business to one another and often making personal phone calls at weekends.

The role of the Prince is destined to become more and more vital over the next decade as Britain moves into Europe and faces bold new challenges

THE EARLY YEARS: Turn to Pages 8 + 9

ARMISTICE DAY: Charles and Diana in Paris

Muriel's run over twice

ELDERLY widow Muriel Millard was feeling the worse for wear yesterday after being run down by a wheelchair ...TWICE!

Muriel, 83, was sent flying on a pedestrian crossing in Bexhill, Sussex. As she lay on the ground the driver, 85-year-old Muriel Ditcham, accidentally put the motorised chair into reverse and hit her namesake again.

A shaken Muriel said: "It will take a long time to get over the shock

Attack on WPC

A POLICE girl was beaten unconscious after being called to a disturbance early yesterday.

WPC Helen Hanson, 22, was taken to hospital following the attack at Norwich. Three policemen were stabbed in the city a week ago.

CAPT. HOOKEY

COMEDIAN Stanley Baxter has pulled out of a new Peter Pan musical at London's Wimbledon Theatre this Christmas after publicity costing thousands of pounds. He is to appear in pantomime in Sunderland instead.

His part of Captain Hook is to be taken by actor Christopher Timothy. He co-stars with Lulu who returns to the stage after her miscarriage earlier this year.

Baxter wanted to be nearer his wife who is ill in Glasgow.

OUT: Baxter

Funeral bust-up

UNDERTAKER Ian Sutherland hit the roof when a traffic warden tried to book him for leaving his hearse outside a church during a funeral at Maidenhead, Berks. Ian had police permission to park on double yellow lines.

DOG FALLS FOR BOOT

A SEXY sheepdog keeps falling in love with farmer Ashley Cridge's wellies.

Ashley, 56, was baffled when five of his boots disappeared from outside his front door in Ellicombe, Somerset.

He found them in a neighbour's haystack after a pal spotted the sheepdog burying one of the boots.

Ashley said: "The dog must have smelt Sandy, our spaniel, on the wellies and fallen in love. I only hope it's a short love affair. I need my boots for work."

Page design

How drugs spelt disaster for David Jenkins

THEY had carved his name with pride in Gateshead. But yesterday the name of David Jenkins was wiped from the record books of his old club.

They called him the Golden Boy of British athletics. But he never struck gold.

They said he would go places. But his short cut to success led only to shame. Yesterday he served the first full day of a seven-year sentence for his key role in a multi-million-dollar drug ring which supplied athletes with fake body-building anabolic steroids.

He went to his cell with the cold words of San Diego judge J. Lawrence Irving for company.

"You have it all, then enters greed and the whole thing seems to go down the toilet," he said.

Jenkins had a first-rate mind in a first-rate body. But he was corrupted by the naked desire to grab as much as quickly as possible — and damn everyone along the way.

Changed

As a youngster he had the world at his feet. He won the European 400 metres title at only 19, and bar one minor race was not beaten over the distance by a Briton until the race that changed his life.

After his European triumph he looked a certain medal-winner in the 1972 Munich Olympics.

But he failed to qualify for the final, though he helped to win a silver for Britain in the relay.

It was a bitter defeat — and Jenkins began his search for a magic ingredient to turn him into a champion.

He took up weight training and read up on physiology. He restructured his training scientifically.

The laboratory offered surer victory than the lonely roads and daily grind.

But that short cut to success was a failure. He finished seventh in the 400 metres in the next two Olympics.

He could have been

the best 400 metres runner the world has seen," said John Anderson, who first spotted his talent.

But the young Trinidad-born athlete who ran his first 400 in 1968 and made the British team within a year turned to drugs before he could prove it.

In an interview six months ago he admitted taking steroids as a young athlete. Despite his failures he could not ditch them.

"It wasn't the drugs," he insisted. "Psychologically I was in a mess. That's why I failed."

So after the 1980 Moscow Olympics Jenkins retired and moved to California. But the search for gold went on.

Drugs had not made him a winner on the

track. But they could do wonders for his bank balance.

He formed links in the seedy Mexican border town of Tijuana and stepped into a drug ring smuggling banned body-building steroids into the United States.

Using a laboratory in the fly-blown township, Jenkins poured steroids into America.

Cancer

In one year his operation smuggled 40 tons of the drugs across the border.

His "little wonders" have been linked to liver cancer, hypertension and heart disease.

They cause shrinkage of sex organs, masculinisation of women and skin diseases.

Daily Mirror investigations revealed that Jenkins's drugs were potentially even more deadly.

Some were for veterinary use only. And they contained vastly varying amounts of steroids.

"Athletes were pumping all sorts of Jenkins's junk into their bodies." U.S. attorney Phil Halpern told us.

But the Golden Boy shrugged his shoulders and counted his share of

the £55 million-a-year business.

He was nailed after a two-year investigation.

Within two months his wife Carol had left him. Jason, the son he adores, will grow from a baby to a boy without him.

GRIFFIN'S EYE

Fool's gold

by ANTON ANTONOWICZ and BARRY WIGMORE

END OF A LONG ROAD

Drug-runner David Jenkins dodges questions as he heads for the cells.

Jenkins faces eventual deportation and bankruptcy.

A mystery golden-haired woman cried in court as he was led away.

She is the only gold left in his life — a life ruined in pursuit of fool's gold.

"It would have been better if I hadn't used drugs," Jenkins told the *Daily Mirror.*

"I succumbed to the pressures because I'm a weak sonabitch. Take the steroids, take the money.

"I wish I hadn't. But I did."

Some like it hot . .

BOOKSELLER Keith Hardy ordered a guide to the Greek holiday island of Lesbos — and was sent a porn book about lesbianism.

Keith, of Bridgwater, Somerset, said: "I don't think it was what the customer had in mind.

It's one of the pitfalls of the job."

MORE LIBEL CASH FOR UNION CHIEF

UNION leader Ron Todd yesterday won "substantial" libel damages from Today newspaper over a report accusing him of a fraud cover-up.

His High Court victory came just a month after he was awarded undisclosed damages against the Sun over allegations of robbery, intimidation and sabotage.

SLUR: Todd

Bingo mum wins big jackpot No 2

BINGO-MAD Jeanette Crawford, who won £38,000 eight months ago, has done it again. Jobless Jeanette scooped the £43,000 first prize at the club in Liscard, Wirral, where she plays seven days a week.

Jeanette spends £40 a week — most of her State benefit — on bingo. She reckons she was nearly covering the lay-out with regular small wins . . . until her two jackpots in a national computer-linked game.

Mother-of-three Jeanette, 39, bought a house with her first big prize. She plans to share the latest win with a bingo pal.

BEATLE'S PAPER ROUND LEGACY

A COUPLE who once lent shivering paper boy Paul McCartney a coat will soon be quids in.

Six years later Paul popped into John and Margaret's sub-post office in Liverpool with a signed photograph of the Beatles. Now they plan to auction the picture and give the cash to their three children.

NEWSBOY: Paul

Killer on the tree

CHRISTMAS candles could be a killer, consumer watchdogs warned yesterday.

Some imported candles come in packs showing them attached to Christmas trees.

But this could lead to a fatal blaze, said trading standards officers in Avon and Dorset.

Page design

PAGE 6 DAILY MIRROR, *Tuesday, November 8, 1988*

Stand by for a topsy-turvy time on the telly

THE biggest shake-up in the history of television is all set to transform our viewing habits . . . and spark a storm about programme quality.

The ITV companies will be up for grabs to the highest bidders at the start of 1992. And few of them expect to survive the switch.

The long-term future of British television has been the subject of speculation since the first hints were dropped of the content of yesterday's Government White Paper on broadcasting.

But what is worrying many people is what will happen to TV programmes before the change takes place.

For the next four years our ITV programmes will be produced by people who confidently expect to be put out of business.

And that is a frightening prospect.

by HILARY BONNER
Showbusiness Editor

Companies without a future are not likely to spend much money producing quality TV.

Expensive home-produced ITV drama like the *Jewel in the Crown* and *Brideshead Revisited* are already a thing of the past.

Now even American co-productions of dubious merit like *The Woman He Loved* starring Jane Seymour and Anthony Andrews may be under threat.

No ITV company until after 1992 is going to take risks or spend money without a certainty of a quick return.

London Weekend Television is unlikely to take another gamble like *Piece of Cake*.

Cheap

And if someone presented Thames with another *Jack the Ripper* tomorrow it would probably seem like too much trouble.

For the next four years we can expect ITV programmes that are either safe or cheap — and preferably both.

Repeats and new series of old and modestly-budgeted favourites like *Bust* and *Shelley* will remain part of our staple diet.

Quiz and games shows like *Blind Date* and *Bullseye* and soaps will not be under threat.

But anything new, anything original, will not happen.

The Government promises that eventually we will have more choice.

There will be a fifth and possibly a sixth major TV channel as well as up to 30 small local city television stations.

And the Home Secretary has pledged that in spite of the emphasis on big money, standards will be maintained.

A quota of news and current affairs and regional programmes will be insisted on.

Indecency and violence will be even more strictly controlled by the new Independent Television Commission and the Broadcasting Standards Council.

And, says the Government, viewers will be given a more direct say.

Only after 1992 will we really know if this will come true or if, as the pessimists forecast, it will all be American-style super-commercialism and more of the same rubbish.

When ITV was launched 33 years ago its brief was that it should "inform, educate and entertain." Today that is history.

The smaller independent companies are already fighting shy of spending money, and quality regional documentaries and current affairs programmes are being scrapped.

The future of the BBC is also in the balance with a gradual phasing out of the licence.

It is the BBC, with its greater stability, that has recently been producing the bulk of our first-class original programmes.

This includes shows like *Fortunes of War* and *First Born*, and comedy, like *Bread*.

And it has always been the BBC, with its emphasis on quality rather than profits, that has helped so much in keeping up the standards of British TV.

The big chiefs at the BBC, faced with demands that they should develop subscription and hand over some of their night hours to a commercial station, are naturally uneasy.

But at least the BBC's existence is not under threat.

Limbo

Each ITV company faces extinction through outsiders outbidding it.

And it is quite extraordinary that this should be so clearly laid on the line four years before being put into operation.

We can expect nothing but a winding-down during this limbo period.

And that's something about which all of us should take a dim view.

● **Today's TV — see Pages 18 and 19.**

GRIFFIN'S EYE

"Hey Margaret! Get on these! They're terrific — they make old age pensioners look wealthy."

The BIG switch

GLOOMY PICTURE: Quality shows like *Piece of Cake* and *Jack the Ripper* could be for the chop.

TWIN WINS A PAY-OUT

AN eight-year-old boy who was brain damaged at birth when doctors failed to realise that his mother was having twins won £350,000 damages in the High Court yesterday.

Darren Slater, of Maidstone, Kent, now needs constant care and supervision because he suffered lack of oxygen in the hour's delay after his twin sister Emma was born. The agreed damages are being paid by health chiefs of the hospital which admitted liability.

£1m for an acre

BUILDERS are now paying around £1million an acre for land in the South East.

The shortage of land there will push up the cost of new homes still further, the Housebuilders Federation warned yesterday.

NOTHING NEW

A TIME capsule buried in hospital foundations by the Queen Mother 60 years ago showed yesterday that times don't change.

When schoolchildren opened the sealed glass jar at a ceremony in Islington, North London, they found a note saying that a new wing at the Fever Hospital had been delayed through lack of cash. The capsule was found by workmen demolishing the building earlier this year. It will now be displayed at Hackney museum.

Queen Mother

Firework boy dies

A TEENAGER who suffered serious burns when a firework set foam-filled furniture ablaze in his bedroom died in hospital yesterday.

Mark Ashley, 14, was trapped on the second floor of his home at Clifton, Nottingham.

DRUG RAID: MAN HELD

A PERUVIAN businessman appeared in court yesterday on charges connected with a £5 million cocaine haul seized by police at the weekend.

Company director Rene Black, 34, of Cranleigh, Surrey, was remanded in custody for a week by Guildford magistrates. He was handcuffed to a prison officer in the dock.

His father-in-law Ronald Fisher, 51, of Dorking, Surrey, was also earlier remanded in custody.

▶ Page design

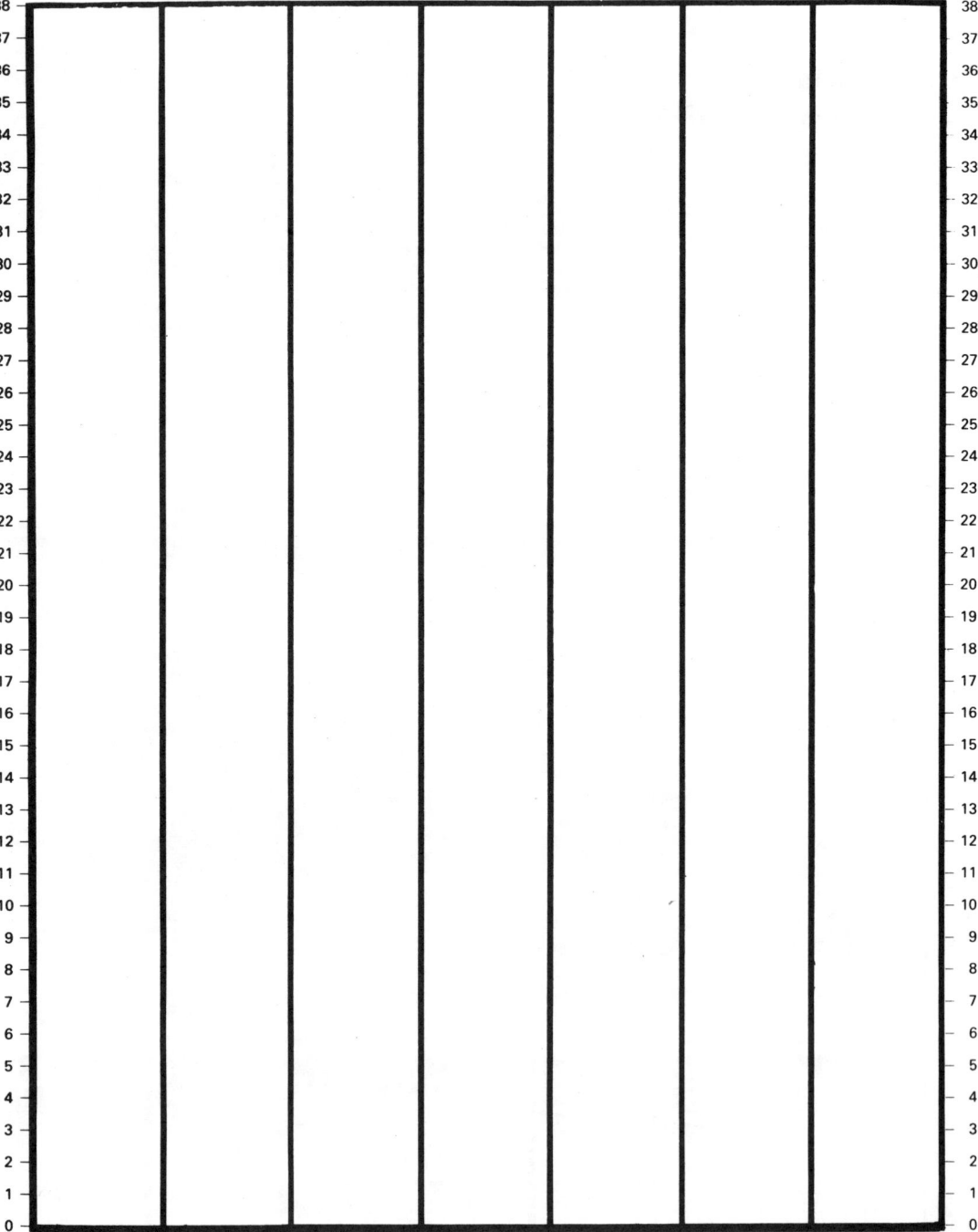

The basic formula

Aim To study how news stories are structured and to practise the skill of structuring a news story

Newspaper stories are written to a set formula. They contain information that answers the questions: **Who? What? Why? Where? When? How?** The story below has been analysed for you.

NUKE CLOUD OVER NORTH

A NUCLEAR cloud with nine times the normal amount of radiation has swept over the North West.

The cloud covered Greater Manchester, Lancashire, Yorkshire and parts of Merseyside a fortnight ago.

Last night the Environment Department denied there had been a cloud or any rise in radiation.

But monitors at sites near Wigan, Greater Manchester and Southport, Lancashire, recorded the high readings and environmental groups took samples from air conditioning units the next day to identify the cloud's origins.

William Peden of the Nuclear Transport Information Group, said: "This was not a natural phenomenon. There was probably an accident on a nuclear submarine in the Irish Sea."

Today 9.11.88

What *is the story about?* Radiation

Where *did it happen?* In the north-west of England

Why *did it happen?* It was probably caused by an accident on a nuclear submarine in the Irish Sea.

Who *found out about it?* Environmental groups

How *did they find out?* They took samples from air conditioning units.

When *did it happen?* 'A fortnight ago'

The basic formula

With your partner, try to analyse these stories in the same way. Use the grid to help you

FLYING SUPERTOT

TODDLER Oliver Hall boasted to his pals yesterday that he could fly like his favourite cartoon character, SuperTed.

Moments later the four-year-old plunged 20ft from his bedroom window — and escaped unhurt.

His mother Pamela said at home in Denmead, Hants: "I looked outside and he was lying in the garden crying. I screamed to my husband to call an ambulance and they rushed him to hospital for X-rays, but there wasn't even a scratch on him."

Mrs Hall added: "I think I'll have to stop him watching SuperTed . . . and get some locks put on the windows."

Daily Mirror 9.11.88

	Supertot	*Alive!*
Who?		
What?		
Where?		
Why?		
How?		
When?		

Alive! A girl with no heart

A BABY girl has lived for a week without her heart beating.

Now it is working again and she is well on the road to recovery.

The baby, nine-month-old Paola Marongiu, underwent surgery in a hospital near Milan to correct a heart defect.

The operation was successful, but Paola's heart stopped beating soon afterwards.

Doctors implanted two mechanical pumps in her chest to circulate her blood while the heart slowly recovered from the strain of the surgery.

Seven days later, it started beating again and the pumps were disconnected.

Paola's case is a medical "first".

Her mother Vincenzina said yesterday: "It's a miracle.

"The doctors say that Paola could be home in time for Christmas. That would be the greatest gift in the world."

Daily Mirror 9.11.88

The basic formula

Now try writing your own news stories using the same formula.

Interview your partner and ask about a time when they won a prize or had an accident or achieved something special.

Make sure you are accurate with the facts. Spell your partner's name correctly, for instance, and make sure that any place names are accurate.

You can vary the questions and ask more than one question for each category.

The interview might go something like this:

Who are you? *Angela Kidd*

What have you achieved? *I won a medal for gymnastics.*

What did you have to do to win the medal? *I took part in a competition.*

Where was the competition held? *At the local sports centre.*

Who took part? *People from all over the county.*

How many? *About fifty.*

How did you feel about winning? *I was surprised but very pleased.*

Who helped you most? *My schoolteacher. Miss Harris the gym teacher. She trained me.*

When did this happen? *Last week.*

When did you take up an interest in gymnastics? *Since I saw a programme on the television about the Olympics.*

Why did that have an effect on you? *Because the gymnasts were so exciting to watch and I wanted to be like them.*

Once you have collected the information, you can then write up the story. Put the main point in the first paragraph and try to include one quotation. Make up a headline.

 Keep the stories for a local interest page in your newspaper.

© John Price, 1991. Newspapers. Macmillan English.
Copyright restrictions on page ii.

TASK
2 # Deciding what is relevant

Aim To practise making decisions about what is important in a news story

When a reporter writes a news story he or she has to decide which facts are important and which are not. The final story is written with the most important facts first and the least important last. This is so that the story can be cut from the bottom upwards without losing vital information. Stories have to be cut sometimes because there is not enough room for them in the paper. This structure is sometimes called 'the inverted pyramid'.

Here are some facts that a reporter collected for a story. Cross out the ones that are really unimportant and number the others in order of importance. (1 means most important, 2 next most important and so on.)

Branson said, 'It's the last great ballooning challenge'.

The balloon is red.

Branson has a beard.

Richard Branson and Per Linstrand are planning to cross the Pacific in a hot air balloon.

The fabric of the balloon is seven miles in length but it is as thin as a £5 note.

The journey should take up to five days.

They will cruise at 11,000 metres.

It will be the largest balloon ever made.

The balloon could hold up to 12,000 parked minis.

The balloon is built by Thunder and Colt of Shropshire.

The balloon is 40ft taller than Nelson's column.

They will go from Japan to the West Coast of the USA.

They will fly 10,000 km on the longest balloon flight in history.

Deciding what is relevant

Now compare your decisions with the version printed in *Scoop*.

Virgin Atlantic boss Richard Branson and balloonist Per Lindstrand are off on another amazing adventure. They're planning to cross the Pacific Ocean in a gigantic hot air balloon!

The dynamic duo will fly 6,200 miles (10,000 km) eastwards over the vast ocean on the longest flight in history.

The trip, from Japan to the West coast of the USA, will more than double their world record distance flight over the Atlantic two years ago.

Branson said it is 'the last great ballooning challenge.'

Their November flight will be in the largest balloon ever built. It stands more than 12 metres taller than Nelson's Column and could hold 12,000 parked minis!

8 miles high!

The adventure should take three to five days, and they'll cruise at a height of 11,500 metres – that's an astonishing eight miles high!

The balloon has been built by Thunder and Colt in Shropshire with new technology developed for this amazing adventure.

Its fabric covers seven miles in length and yet is just the thickness of a £5 note!

Scoop 12.10.89

Look again at the story you wrote about your partner in Task 1 of this Assignment. Redraft it, starting with the most important information and ending with the least important information, so that it could be cut from the bottom upward without losing any vital information.

On 26 November 1989, the Branson dream of a fantastic balloon flight was shattered when the balloon blistered and collapsed from the heat of the burners, due to faulty construction. Richard Branson vowed he would try again next year ...

Lead paragraphs

Aim To practise writing lead paragraphs for news stories

A news story always has its main point in the first paragraph. The reason for this is that people read newspapers quickly and they need to know if a story is worth spending time over. The reporter's job is to grab the reader's attention which he or she does by writing a short, snappy opening.

Look at the lead paragraphs shown on Sheet 17. They are in groups of three, each group dealing with a different story. Discuss which are the most effective lead paragraphs and give reasons for your choice.

Now try to write your own lead paragraphs.

Think of five nursery stories, such as Red Riding Hood, and write the lead paragraphs in the style of a news story.

For example:

> A bed-ridden granny has been savagely attacked by a wolf at an isolated cottage in the woods.

Choose one of your lead paragraphs and then write the whole story. (Maximum of 200 words.)

 Keep your stories for your group newspaper.

© John Price, 1991. Newspapers. Macmillan English.
Copyright restrictions on page ii.

Lead paragraphs

Four sailors amazingly survived FOUR MONTHS at sea clinging to the top of their capsized yacht.

EXPERTS IN New Zealand are calling the voyage of the Rose-Noelle one of the most remarkable stories ever told of survival at sea.

INVESTIGATORS are checking out an amazing claim of survival on the high seas.

Britain's death rate for young pedestrians is one of the worst in Europe – with more than 20,000 youngsters killed or injured every year.

SCHOOLS and road planners are blasted in a new report for failing to act to end the scandal of child deaths on the streets.

Almost half the accidents on urban roads involve child pedestrians according to a new report by the AA. More than 800 under-15's died in road accidents and many thousands required hospital treatment last year.

NOT ALL East Germans were celebrating the 40th birthday of their country last weekend. Despite severe travel restrictions, and despite a police crackdown, thousands of East Germans were fleeing their communist homeland in search of a better life in the West.

THE turmoil goes on in Communist East Europe, with police beating rioting crowds in East Germany.

Thousands of East Germans are flooding to the West to escape Communism. More than 30,000 have fled in the last two months hoping to make new lives in West Germany.

© John Price, 1991. *Newspapers*, Macmillan English.
Copyright restrictions on page ii.

TASK 2 Key words

Aim To learn how the word order in opening sentences can be used to stress key words

Even when a lead paragraph has been selected, the writer has to decide which words in the opening sentence he or she needs to emphasise. These key words are placed at the beginning of the sentence.

Here are four ways of writing the same information, but each one stresses something different:

- Two boy muggers, aged seven, savagely attacked an old woman on her way to church.
- A savage attack on an old woman on her way to church was made by two boy muggers, aged seven.
- An old woman on her way to church was savagely attacked by two seven-year-old boy muggers.
- On her way to church an old woman was savagely attacked by two seven-year-old boy muggers.

Discuss which version emphasises the most important information in your opinion. Which bit of the story is the most significant?

Re-write these opening sentences so that the key words come at the beginning of each one.

- A fire was prevented from causing serious injury yesterday because little Clare Brown raised the alarm.
- There has been growing concern about the risk of salmonella in eggs and the government are planning a national campaign to reduce the risks of food poisoning.
- Four people hijacked a Briton's yacht and detectives are waiting to interview the Briton because the four died when the yacht exploded and sank.
- Exhaust fumes from cars have been trapped by fog in London and a huge cloud of poisonous gas threatens the city.
- It costs £900, almost ten times as much as existing drugs, for a new wonder drug that could save thousands of lives, so doctors are in a dilemma.

TASK

3 Headline writing

Aim To practise writing headlines in different styles

Newspapers use headlines because of the way that papers are read by the public. Most people do not spend a long time reading a paper. About twenty minutes is the average reading time. Readers need to be able to select quickly the bits of the paper that are of interest to them.

Headlines label stories so that people can tell quickly if they want to read a particular story.

> *How to write a good headline*
> 1 Emphasise the main point of a story.
> 2 Use as few words as possible.
> 3 Use a particular style (see below)

There are several different styles of newspaper headline. Collect and display examples of the following headline styles.

Write as many different styles of headline as you can for this story:

FIVE potholers trapped for 12 hours in a flooded cave were criticised by their rescuers yesterday.

Chief Inspector Brian Andrews said: "There is no way they should have gone down in the first place.

He added: "The cave is prone to rapid flooding and when it rained that should have been sufficient warning."

The five, all experienced potholers from Sheffield, huddled on two narrow stone ledges when a flash flood sent thousands of gallons of water pouring into Deluge Pot on the Yorkshire Dales. Separating the two ledges was a raging 35ft waterfall.

Rescuers had to divert a flooded stream inside the 220ft deep cave before moving in to lead the potholers to safety.

Three men were brought out first. It was another two hours before Michelle Riley, 22, and David Crowther, 37, could be led to the surface.

Today 20.12.88 Ahil Crampes

▶ Headline writing

Alliteration

FLORAL FINALE AT FIREWORK FESTIVAL

Exclamations

OUTCLASSED!

Headlines balanced around a preposition

Top Award for Brave Hero

Local School Head in Fierce Race Row

Puns

Stolen Lamp Came to Light

Informative

Tube Blaze May Have Killed 32

Sensational

L.A. Law Hunk Shops as Wife Gives Birth in Aisle

Colloquial

Minister's brother sold me duff motor!

Headline character counts

Aim To learn how to write headlines to fit limited space

One of the jobs a sub-editor on a newspaper does it to design headlines not just to give concise information, but to fit a given space on a page. This means thinking in terms of the numbers of characters on separate lines.

The task is complicated a little bit by the fact that a space as well as a letter counts as a character. Moreover, two letters, 'w' and 'm', have a character count of $1\frac{1}{2}$, because they take more space than other letters, while 'i' and 'l' only count as $\frac{1}{2}$ characters because they are thin.

Copter Search For
Mother On The Run

In this headline the balance between the lines of the headline is good, and both lines fit within the column allowed for the text. The character count is 17 in the first line (15 letters and 2 spaces) and $17\frac{1}{2}$ in the second line ($14\frac{1}{2}$ letters plus 1.5 for the 'm' and 3 spaces).

Helicopter Search For
Runaway Mum

This version creates an imbalance between the lines, and the top line is too wide for the text column.

Helicopter Search
for Missing Mum

This headline has a better balance between its lines, but does it tell you as much as the others?

▶ Headline character counts

Headline writers therefore need to have a good vocabulary so they can choose words of different lengths without altering meaning. This is why they often use short words instead of long ones, such as 'quiz' instead of 'interrogate' in the headline:

Police To Quiz Suspect

Write two or three headlines for each of the following stories. Make sure that the headline has roughly the same number of characters in each line and that it fills the space available. For greater accuracy, use a word processor if one is available.

Story One:

POLICE are hunting a masked raider who got away with cash in a lunchtime raid on a city centre bank today.

The man burst into the Citicentre Bank in Green Street at 12.10 and demanded money from a cashier. He said he was armed and would shoot to kill.

The terrified cashier handed over £260 in £10 notes to the robber, who fled.

Detectives today released a description of the man they want to trace.

He is in his early thirties, around 5ft 4in tall and was wearing a camouflage jacket. He had a mask covering the bottom part of his face. He had a local accent.

Story Two:

TWO youths tried to escape capture by jumping over a bridge after a factory break-in, a court was told today.

Police were chasing a van, which had been used in the break-in, when it stopped and two youths jumped over the side of a motorway bridge onto the central reservation below.

The police caught both youths. One was unconscious and the other was trying to limp away.

The youths admitted the break-in, during which a safe was damaged and £650 was stolen, and were put on probation for two years.

Story Three:

THE war against litter louts is hotting up. A major TV campaign is to be launched to highlight the social problems caused by litter. The adverts will hammer home the message that the public must keep the environment clean.

The Tidy Britain Group is to ask for government funding to start the campaign, but private firms will be expected to help out too.

One advert shows a dog cutting its nose on a jagged can which has been thrown into the gutter. Another shows a toddler falling onto broken glass.

A Tidy Group spokesman said: "We aim to shock people into doing something about the growing menace to our lives of dangerous litter."

Story Four:

BRITAIN'S MPs are bottom of the class when it comes to environment issues.

Many of them have not a clue when it comes to topics like deforestation, lead-free petrol and the ozone layer, says a survey conducted by *The Sunday Times.*

Of 75 MPs who were asked some simple questions about the environment, only twelve got them all right, nearly half got two or more wrong and one got 0 out of 5!

Interviews

Aim To understand how journalists use interviews to compile stories

A reporter has to decide which people have important information or opinions about a story. The reporter then has to persuade these people to give the facts or express their opinions and record them accurately.

Read Kevin O'Lone's article Teachers slam the strike it rich shows.

- What did Peter Dawson say that gave O'Lone the starting point of his story?
- What job does Peter Dawson do that makes his opinions important and influential?
- List the other people that O'Lone interviewed and say why their jobs make their views important.
- If you were writing the story would you have interviewed any other people to get a different angle?

▶ Interviews

Teachers slam the 'strike it rich' quiz shows

SLAMMED: *Trick Or Treat.*

SLAMMED: *Jim Bowen's Bullseye.*

CHILDREN'S minds are being warped by the promise of big prizes in game-show-crazy Britain. That's the charge levelled at TV today.

A teachers' union says the boom in shows such as *Strike It Lucky, The Price Is Right, Trick Or Treat, Wheel Of Fortune* and *Bullseye* is helping to spawn a generation of "strike-it-rich" kids who expect easy pickings in life.

Watching as contestants are showered with rewards is turning youngsters into grasping consumers who know the price of everything and the value of nothing, it claims.

But *Bullseye* host Jim Bowen has hit back angrily. He reckons teachers, not game shows, are to blame if kids are not interested in working in class.

The latest attack on prize shows comes from the Professional Association of Teachers.

At its annual conference in Birmingham this week it will debate a motion deploring the "lavish prizes given away on game shows for the poor example set to young children."

by KEVIN O'LONE

Diet

PAT general secretary Peter Dawson said yesterday: "It's becoming increasingly difficult for teachers to get pupils to work for the satisfaction of achievement.

"Youngsters are fed an unremitting diet of game and quiz shows on television and are growing up with warped values.

"They think life is like a game show — that you can get something for nothing."

But Jim Bowen last night rejected the PAT complaint.

He said: "I am sick and tired of the patronising attitude of teachers.

"If they're worried about motivating children, then they can't be much good as teachers.

"I don't think because youngsters see someone win a holiday or a microwave oven they're going to think they don't have to work at school.

"Contestants have to pass a stiff test and some of the questions are very difficult.

"Television is one of the greatest teaching aids known to man."

The PAT motion has been put forward by Hull primary school teacher Phil Withers. He says: "Some of the shows do have educational value but in many the only point is to win a prize.

"Many pupils grow up expecting to walk straight into a fully-furnished home, complete with Teasmaid, toaster and colour TV.

The hysteria of the audience is probably the most harmful influence."

Peter Dawson says: "Pupils spend huge amounts of time watching television, sometimes until midnight.

"They turn up for school in the morning stupefied. And the favourite programmes seem to be game or quiz shows.

"The level of knowledge expected in them is pathetic.

"It is one of the things which have teachers lying awake at night worrying."

But their fears are groundless, says Steve Leahy, TV's Mr Game Show".

Limit

Steve is the man who devised or produced many of the game shows on the box, including *Wheel Of Fortune* and *Busman's Holiday*. He said: "Peter Dawson is a spoilsport with no sense of humour.

"Game and quiz shows are light entertainment and the prizes are not just thrown away. Some of the questions are very difficult.

"The Independent Broadcasting Authority has set a limit of £6,000 per show on prizes, so you're not going to win a fortune."

A BBC spokeswoman said the Corporation did not offer lavish prizes. She added: "We would reject any suggestion that any BBC programme creates a climate of greed or envy"

Steve agrees: "You don't need prize-money for game shows to be successful — the game's the thing.

"Britain is just beginning to go game-show crazy.

"We're doing *Wheel Of Fortune* for Scottish Television and we've had 30,000 applications to go on the show.

"Quiz shows are one of the few forms of TV which generate participation. I'm sure we've all watched them and shouted out answers and picked up things we didn't know before.

"Isn't THAT learning?"

The price is too high
WATCH IT
Britain is going overboard for shows like Michael Barrymore's *Strike It Lucky.*

Daily Mirror 31.7.89

Conducting your own interviews

Aim To collect and use information from interviews as the basis for a newspaper story

Take a controversial talking point as a starting point for your story. For instance, the chair of the school governors has said, 'Television is a harmful influence on pupils and parents should ration or even ban TV watching so that children can concentrate on reading and doing their homework'.

Interview several people who have opinions on this topic. Look for people who express different points of view.

You can do this for real or as a role-play exercise. If you do it as a role-play, get people in the class to be some of the following:

the chairman of the governors   *teachers*
a representative of the education   *the local MP*
   department of the local TV station   *local religious leaders*
parents   *employers*

Make sure that people have time to work out their reasons and arguments *before* you interview them.

Tape record the interviews if possible and then select the main points from the interviews and quote them accurately in an article on the issue. Try to balance your article so that you give equal weight to opposing views. Do not give your own opinions.

Some other starting points:

- The leader of an environmental group has said that the time has come to ban private cars from city centres because of the pollution they cause.

- The leader of an educational pressure group has called for the return of single sex schools because it has been shown that girls learn science and technology more effectively when they are not grouped with boys.

- The local council want to ban dogs from their parks because of the health hazards to young children.

 Keep your articles for your group newspaper.

TASK 3 'The Rescue'

Aim To compile a newspaper report based on information collected in interviews

You have been sent to investigate a report of a brave rescue of a boy who was drowning in the sea. You have a tape recorder with you and you interview several people. Here are some extracts from the transcript of your tape recording.

Write a report of the incident using some of the quotations you have collected. Make sure you put quotation marks round the words actually spoken. Write about 300 words and supply a headline. Begin your story with straightforward reporting, for example: *Two boys were saved from drowning yesterday when a passer-by jumped into the sea and dragged them to safety.*

▶ Joy Revel: eye witness
I was walking along the promenade with my boyfriend when we heard a shout. We looked up and saw someone in the water waving his arms. He kept going under. I think he must have fallen into the sea from the pier where he had been fishing. One of his friends jumped in but he was not a strong swimmer and he started to struggle. My boyfriend ran to phone for help. It was all very frightening.

▶ Alan Boyd: tried to rescue friend
We were fishing from the pier and everything was OK, but suddenly there was a huge wave that swept over us. Tony lost his balance and just got dragged into the sea. He is a good swimmer, but he couldn't get back to the pier. I didn't think; I just jumped in to try to help him. The current was so strong it was just forcing us both out to sea and trying to pull us under. However hard you tried to swim it was no good. I was powerless.

▶ Tony Slater: boy who nearly drowned
This huge wave came and just knocked me flat. There was nothing I could do to stop myself going over the edge and into the sea. At first I thought I could save myself, but the current was too strong. When

'The Rescue'

Alan jumped in, he grabbed hold of me, but I could soon tell that he was in trouble too. Then this other lad came along and dived in. He was a really strong swimmer and he put a proper lifesaver's hold on me and got me to the pier again. Then he went back and helped Alan.

I haven't seen him since to thank him but I owe him my life.

▶ Mark Stebbings: rescuer
It was just sheer chance that I happened to be there at the time. I don't normally go anywhere near the beach at this time of the year. I am a qualified lifesaver and I work at the local swimming pool. I didn't think twice about going in to help the lads who were in trouble. No I don't think of myself as a hero. I don't want any fuss made. I just did what anyone else would have done.

▶ Police spokesperson:
There was a report of an incident at the South Pier. An ambulance was called and two fifteen-year-old boys were taken to St Margaret's Hospital. An officer was sent to the scene of the incident and interviewed some eye-witnesses. We do not suspect any foul play.

It seems that one boy was swept from the pier into the sea and another two members of the public were involved in rescue attempts. We are investigating complaints that the pier is not a safe place for fishing.

▶ Mrs Slater: mother of boy who nearly drowned
It's about time the council did something about that pier. It is not safe for fishing. There should be a sign to tell people it is dangerous. I've told Tony time and time again to keep away but he takes no notice.

▶ Mrs Stebbings: mother of Mark
I'm very proud of Mark. It's just the kind of thing he would do. He has always been very daring. He once rescued a cat from a burning building.

TASK 4

'No Cause, No Cure'

Aim To understand how journalists personalise stories and to write a personalised story

Journalists are trained to 'hang a story on a person'. They may be given a topic to write about which is very general, such as the plight of the Vietnamese refugees in Hong Kong. They try to help the ordinary reader to understand the problem by focusing on one particular family and telling their story. In this way readers can relate the problem to their own lives.

Read 'No Cause, No Cure' on Sheet 29. This was a feature in the *Star* on a page which also reviewed the film *Rain Man*, a story about someone suffering from autism.

Write down you views on the following:

- How does the writer 'hang the story on a person'?
- What does the article tell you about autism?

Discuss with your partner how you could personalise the following stories:

Topic	Ways of personalising
Competitive sports in schools	*What it's like to be a winner; the people who opt out; the problems PE teachers have in motivating people*

Enterprise education

Bullying

River pollution

Healthy eating

Local football team wins FA cup

Poverty

Prejudice

Choose your preferred example and write it up on your own as a personalised story.

 Keep it for your group newspaper.

▶ 'No Cause, No Cure'

NO CAUSE, NO CURE

The torment of being Brian . . .

EXTRA SPECIAL . . . Like any lively 4-year-old

RAIN MAN is a worthy, potential Oscar-winning film—but it may obscure the fact that not every autistic child is particularly gifted.

Take four-year-old Brian. He looked bright as a button on ITV's Find A Family series.

Like all the other kids in the televised adoption campaign, he simply wanted a brand new mum and dad to look after him.

And, despite his extra-special needs, more than 250 people called to say they would give him the love, attention and painstaking help an autistic youngster demands.

Kisses

Yet Brian's case still highlights the tremendous pressure that is exerted on parents of such children.

With great reluctance, his natural mother and father gave him up because they were unable to cope.

He has been with foster parents for the last two years. But now, with another baby of their own on the way and other children to look after, they feel he needs a more permanent home.

"Brian can understand very simple words and he can give kisses . . . when he feels like it," says social worker Lesley Henderson.

Sadly Brian won't mix with other children.

"It's frightening for children his age who want to play with him when he screams," says Lesley.

"The kind of progress he will make will be in very small steps."

Brian has learned to drink from a cup and feed himself. He now enjoys outings in the car.

Handicap

"But there's no such thing as a typical autistic child," Lesley stresses.

Only a handful of Britain's 80,000 autistics are gifted.

All simply have one thing in common . . . a lifelong mental handicap for which no cause nor cure is known.

And a new parent might not even recognise autism in their child because they make so few demands.

It is only AFTER diagnosis that warning signs—such as lack of sense of danger, preference for objects rather than people and seeming deafness—make any sense.

As one mother told the National Autistic Society: "I think I'd rather have a normal, abnormal child . . ; if you know what I mean."

The Star 6.3.89

News and features

Aim To work out a definition of a feature article

The 'A' extracts printed here and on Sheet 31 are from news stories, while those marked 'B' are from feature articles. With your partner, talk about the differences between the two groups and decide on a definition of a feature article.

B1
CONVINCED that neither Britain nor France would fight Nazi Germany, Josef Stalin, the Soviet leader signed a non-aggression pact with Hitler on August 23.

The alliance between the arch enemies of fascism and communism was a sensational development. It shocked the world and destined Europe onto the final lap towards war.

Early Times 10.9.89

A1
THE SAINSBURY'S Young Cook of the Britain competition took place this week. There were contestants from all over the country. Julia Noon, 12, the North of England finalist from Lancashire who cooked Filo Basket Parisienne followed by Pear Politique Delight, said: "I would like to meet the Prime Minister because she seems nice towards children. Being so busy it must be difficult to have something prepared using her favourite foods." Mrs Thatcher was not one of the judges.

The Indy 19.10.89

A2
PUPILS AT the King Edward School in Birmingham have gone into the record books as the Swots of the Century. They achieved a 95.5 per cent pass rate in their A-Level exams this summer. 120 pupils entered the exams. The headmaster is reported to be very proud.

The Indy 19.10.89

B3
Smoking is Britain's biggest killer. 250 people die in Britain every *day*. They die mainly of lung cancer, their lungs clogged up and destroyed by a thick black treacly tar.

Smoking for many years also causes areas of the lungs to be completely destroyed – a condition known as emphysema.

Scoop 3.9.89

B2
EARTHQUAKES happen when two of the Earth's 12 continental plates slip against each other — releasing untold energy as the Earth's surface tears apart.

The massive plates are in constant motion, too slow for the eye to see, but always driven by currents generated within the planet's super-hot centre.

Sunderland Echo 10.9.89

News and features

A3

Daylight robbery

Bank robber Frank Colella didn't get very far after making off with £1,300 – he was mugged outside the bank! Then poor old Frank reported the mugging to the police – and was promptly slapped in the nick. "Only a psychiatrist would know why he reported it," said the police.

Scoop 3.9.89

A4

PARENTS WHO fail to prevent their children committing crimes are to face heavy financial penalties, under legal changes planned by Douglas Hurd, the Home Secretary.
"The family is our first defence against crime," the minister said. "For too long in this country we have pushed parental responsiblity into the sidelines." The law, he said, "should reinforce the principle that parents have a responsibility for the actions of their children."

The Indy 19.10.89

A5

MORE than 270 people were killed and 500 injured in a massive earthquake which shook San Francisco today.
The quake — on the notorious San Andreas Fault — measured 6.9 on the Richter scale, sparking fires and causing widespread destruction.
Troops are patrolling the streets to arrest looters running riot in the Third Street sector — the city's major crack and cocaine dealing area.

Scoop 3.9.89

B4

FOR thousands of children throughout the world home is a place behind bars and within four prison walls.
But some of these children are being held in prison through no fault of their own - the only crime they or their parents have committed is that they have no home, for in some countries in the world, the law dictates that if a family is found wandering the streets, they must be imprisoned.

Early Times 10.9.89

B5

THIS month marks the 20th anniversary of the decision to use the British army to maintain order in Northern Ireland.
By August 1969 law and order had all but broken down in the Province. Riots, bombings, and burnings had reached such a pitch that the police were unable to guarantee people's safety.
The immediate cause, of what were to be called 'the Troubles', was the demand for increased civil rights by the Province's Catholic population.

Early Times 10.9.89

The feature extract on the San Francisco earthquake (B2) explained how earthquakes occur. What other feature ideas can you think of to back up an earthquake news story?

The specialist feature

Aim To examine and then practise the techniques used in writing specialist feature articles

Read Miriam Stoppard's feature about coping with pain.

Miriam Stoppard is a doctor and television personality. For these two reasons her medical advice features are used by many newspapers. Her challenge is to explain often complex problems in language which the average reader can understand: a specialist writer has to be both a specialist and a good communicator.

Discuss these questions in your groups. They are designed to help you understand the writer's techniques:

- How does Miriam Stoppard make the opening of the article sound as if she is telling a story rather than giving medical information?

- Which particular children are mentioned by name? What effect does this have on the reader?

- How would you describe the style of writing in 'It's important, because how your mum feels affects the way you feel too.' Why has Miriam Stoppard used this style?

- Choose three sentences that show you that Miriam Stoppard understands people's feelings. Why do you think it is important that she does this?

- Explain in no more than 100 words the medical technique that Miriam Stoppard describes.

Now try to use some of these techniques to write your own specialist feature article.

- First, choose a subject that you already know something about.

- Decide which group of people you are writing for and what tone of voice or style will be most suitable for them.

- Select about five main points that you want to tell your readers about.

- Make it sound as though you are telling a story.

- Write about people's feelings if possible.

- Write about named people if you can.

- Involve your readers by asking questions such as 'how does this affect *you*?'

Miriam Stoppard

ONE Tuesday afternoon when filming for the new series of "Where There's Life" I walked on to a children's ward in California to find Sunny giving this doll a spinal tap – but he wasn't just playing.

He's part of a group of children with cancer at the Los Angeles Children's Hospital who are learning to control pain – pain from vital tests needed to monitor the progress of the disease.

Most painful are spinal taps and bone marrow aspirations.

In his Stride

Mikey, another child suffering from leukaemia, was diagnosed last August, and after many visits to hospital he takes treatment in his stride. Today he is receiving anti-cancer drugs through the line permanently installed in his chest.

It wasn't always so easy. Mikey dreaded bone marrow aspiration, where a sample of marrow is removed by pushing a needle right into the bone.

So a child psychologist and her team worked out a way for the children to control their pain.

They discovered that when the children felt helpless and out of control, the pain was more difficult to bear.

Any hospital visit might make a child feel that way, but these procedures were especially bad because the patient has to curl up in a vulnerable position, with their spine exposed, unable to see what is happening behind them, and not knowing when the pain will strike.

So on the day of the bone or spinal tap, the child is shown exactly what will happen to them.

And to make them feel really in charge, they get to be the doctor for a while – even if the patient is only a doll.

All the children in that clinic had cancer, and will have to endure pain at some time.

The researchers have found that children often believe all pain is punishment, and if they think it is their fault, the pain will seem worse.

And the reverse is also true – the pain will actually seem less bad if the child can think of it as something positive – as part of their cure.

So while the children play at giving bone marrows to their rag dolls, Elva the art therapist gets them to talk about it – to find out how they really feel and to make sure they have understood what happens – and why.

It was almost time for Sunny's spinal tap, so he practised relaxation techniques with the co-ordinator, Patricia, who will be there when he does it for real.

But now the rehearsal was over. As Cathy prepared Sunny's back, Patricia and his mother helped him to begin the familiar routine.

Throughout the procedure, Sunny's mum comforted and supported him, not easy when your child is in pain. Many do relaxation exercises themselves to make sure they give their children the best possible help.

It's important, because how your mum feels affects the way you feel too.

Sunny came through the spinal tap with flying colours and without a murmur. For his bravery, he was given a prize, a shiny gold trophy.

Coping positively

By rewards for bravery the L.A. children see pain as something positive, as part of their cure and are better able to cope with it.

It was so impressive seeing those youngsters, they could teach us adults a lot about bearing pain!

Sunderland Echo 25.5.88

- Identify with your readers with statements like 'most of *us.*'

Here are some ideas for you to try:

How to start a particular hobby
Surviving holidays with parents
How to be in the fashion next summer
Organising a sponsored event
How to start a school enterprise
Making the most of your local library
Why CDT has replaced woodwork and metalwork –
a guide for parents

 Save your specialist article for the group newspaper you are compiling.

TASK
1 Writing an editorial

Aim To write an editorial in which you give reasons for your opinion and quote evidence to support it

A newspaper's editorial is written by the editor or some other senior writer. It is written in response to a particular news story. The writer refers to the story briefly and expresses an opinion about it. He or she produces evidence to back that opinion up. Here is a typical editorial from the *Daily Express*

- How does it state the problem and show that it is topical?
- What evidence does it give about the problem?
- What solutions to the problem does it suggest?

Seat belt shame

MORE than 60 children are killed and over 7,000 injured every year through travelling unrestrained in the backs of cars. Those are the alarming official statistics that prompted Mr Stephen Day's Private Member's Bill making it compulsory to have children belted up in cars with rear seat-belts.

The legislation, which comes into effect on the first of next month, and the accompanying £500,000 publicity campaign, will go far to cutting this needless toll. Sadly, the new regulations will do only so much. No more than 35 per cent of cars now have rear seat belts. That means 65 per cent will remain potential deathtraps for young rear passengers.

And not so young passengers. Unbelted adults are also at risk.

Yet adults are not required to wear rear belts even where they are available. Ministers think it wrong to make belt-wearing compulsory while only 35 per cent of cars have them in the rear.

But where's the logic in that? If it is worthwhile to require children to be belted up it must surely be no less worthwhile to have adults belted up too; the percentage of cars fitted with rear belts is the same either way.

Mr Day wanted his Bill to cover both children and adults but was forced, by ministerial pressure, to water down his proposals. The Government's attitude is as short-sighted as it is illogical. Lives that could be saved will be needlessly lost.

However, since Ministers have foolishly passed up the chance to boost the wearing of rear seat belts, motorists — especially those with small children — should take the lead themselves. Those with pre-October 1986 cars should have belts fitted. They should not regard rear belts as an optional extra but as a vital one — a life-saver.

The children, especially, deserve nothing less.

Daily Express 4.8.89

Writing an editorial

Write an editorial about one of the newslines shown below.

Discuss the topics first in small groups so that you get other people's points of view.

Try to justify your opinions by giving evidence or reasons.

BANKS ARE SET TO GIVE CREDIT CARDS TO YOUNGSTERS OVER THE AGE OF NINE AND A NATIONAL RETAIL COMPANY PLANS TO OPEN SPECIAL STORES TO CATER EXCLUSIVELY FOR THE 9 - 16 YEAR OLDS.

A LOCAL AMUSEMENT ARCADE OWNER HAS BANNED GIRLS FROM THE ARCADE HE OWNS BECAUSE THEY 'DISTRACT THE BOYS FROM THE MACHINES'.

THE NUMBER OF PEOPLE SLEEPING ROUGH IN LONDON HAS RISEN BY 50 PER CENT IN A YEAR.

TEACHERS HAVE COMPLAINED THAT SOME OF THEIR PUPILS' PARENTS ARE BEING TOO HELPFUL WITH COURSEWORK. 'SOMETIMES THE KIDS DO NOTHING AT ALL. IT IS ALL THE WORK OF THEIR MUMS AND DADS'.

SCHOOL PUPILS ARE BEING PAID TO STAY BEHIND AND CLEAN UP THEIR CLASSROOMS BECAUSE OF A SHORTAGE OF SCHOOL CLEANERS.

NEW EEC REGULATIONS WILL PREVENT CHILDREN UNDER 16 FROM DOING ANY PAID WORK. THIS WILL MEAN THE END OF PAPER ROUNDS.

 Keep your editorial for your group newspaper.

Styles of editorial

Aim To study an editorial in which humour is used to convey the writer's point of view

Not all editorials are serious. Sometimes writers use humour to make their points. Look at this editorial from the *Daily Mirror*. The topic is the standard of English teaching in schools. This became 'news' after Prince Charles was overheard to say:

> 'All the people in my office, they can't speak properly, they can't write properly. All the letters from my office I have to correct myself. And that is because English is taught so bloody badly. That is the problem.'

MIRROR COMMENT

PRINTS Charlie ain't off his loaf when he says we don't talk or spell proper, though bloody ain't proper, neither, and he and his old pot and pan says that a lot.

Nor is making out his staff are a bunch of Arfur Daleys and Terry Whatsits proper by a long chalk.

It ain't there fault if Eton don't learn them the difference between there articles and there elocution.

But he's dead right, reely.

Proper English ain't taught nowadays. Have a butcher's at what the leaders of the teachers' unions said yesterday.

Worse

One said the Prints was "over the top" and the other said it was a case of "the pot calling the kettle black."

Charlie might have bin a bit out of order, but clitches from teachers is worse than bad spelling from secretaries, innit?

Daily Mirror 29.6.89

The Mirror editorial writer agrees with what Prince Charles said, but makes another point about the English of the teachers' union leaders who responded to the Prince's criticisms.

The style of the piece, however, is ironic, with the deliberate use of 'bad' English. The effect of this is to stop the reader taking the whole thing too seriously.

Re-write the editorial in standard English and talk about what difference this makes to its impact.

TASK 3 Reviews

Aim To write a review of a book, film, record or TV programme

Newspapers review and preview all kinds of things from new films to current art exhibitions. The purpose of the review is partly to summarise the content of the subject, but mainly to express the reviewer's opinion of it. Reviews and previews both guide readers so that they can more easily choose something that they want to see or hear or read from the vast amount of material around them.

Work by yourself and read each of the following reviews carefully. Select from each one the sentence that best expresses the writer's opinion.

- Which review makes you most want to read or see what is being reviewed? Give reasons for your choice.
- Which review do you find most interesting? Why?

 Write your own reviews for your group newspaper. You should combine description and opinion.

Remember me to Harold Square, by **Paula Danziger** (Piper, £2.25) is set in the Big Apple, New York. 14-year-old Kendra Kaye and her brother Oscar meet Frank Lees, who has come to spend the summer with them.

Frank is 15, blonde, six foot tall with blue eyes. Kendra is another set of good things. Bingo! They swear undying felicity and that's it.

Actually the good thing about this book is that it is funny. Kendra and Oscar have a wickedly good sense of humour which makes sure of one thing - it won't be long before Kendra grows out of these six foot tall blondes with blue eyes.

The Indy 12.10.89

The Wonderstuff
Hup
Any record containing the line "beat me up with the pumice stone" cannot be all bad. *30 Years in the Bathroom* is as amusing as it sounds, as are the darker *Cartoon Boyfriend* and *Radio Ass Kiss*. On a couple of the record's twelve tracks, this eight-legged groove machine sounds like it's been bending all its eight ears towards the Waterboys. And that's no bad thing. Laced with samples and sound effects, it's one giant laugh you can dance to.

The Indy 12.10.89

▶ Reviews

A weird language

THIS is my book review of **Mrs Byrne's Dictionary of Unusual Obscure and Preposterous Words.** It is the funniest dictionary you'll ever come across!

Turning the pages of this book words such as *brobdingnagian* meaning enormous and *furfaceous* meaning covered in dandruff, jump out at you. The most amazing thing is that all the words in this book have been accepted by at least one major dictionary as a legitimate part of the English language!

Mrs Byrne's Dictionary would be invaluable for livening up a game of Scrabble, or even for your next English essay.

A couple of *abbuzzos* discreetly dropped in would certainly give

Mairi MacPherson

your English teacher a shock!

This dictionary is a fascinating reference book and a pleasure to dip into again and again. I would thoroughly recommend this book to you if you are interested in language, or you just like a good laugh.

Mrs Byrne's Dictionary of Unusual Obscure and Preposterous Words **is written by Josefa Heifetz Byrne and is published by Granada Publishing. It costs £2.95 in paperback.**

Early Times 10.8.89

TELEVISION

Jeremy Novick taps his feet to his pick of the week

What's that noise?

Let's talk pop. Let's talk music television. What have you got? You've got Top of the Pops. It's there and always was and always will be. But what about music that isn't in the charts? Well, there's Def this, Def that and Def the other. But what do you do if you're not Def?

The problem with most pop on the box is that you've really got no choice. It's already been decided for you, what's hip, what's funky, what's trendy.

Def II ? Dead hip, but what does it mean?

What it means is someone with funky jeans, a funky haircut and a "street" accent telling you about the latest big things with funky jeans, funky haircuts, etc. It's a bit like looking through the windows at a party you haven't been invited to.

Wouldn't it be nice if there was a pop show which didn't

preach.? A show which gave you loads of different types of music and didn't tell you whether they were hip or trendy or any of those other things which don't actually mean anything.

Hey, *What's That Noise*?

What's That Noise? is a new music show, a million miles away from the idea that what's good about your music is your haircut. A thousand miles away from the idea that you cannot possibly have Eartha Kitt, Bronski Beat, Cold Cut, the Reggae Philharmonic Orchestra and the sound engineer from

The Rolling Stones in the same show. *What's That Noise?* has all of those people in one show. Incidentally, in that same show is the Gamelan, a type of music from Bali that has just got to be seen.

Six programmes, each one on a particular theme: Roots, Rythmn, Words, Mood, Controls and Image. In the Rythmn show you go from Cliff Richard to the Cheetham Music School (playing a Strauss waltz), taking in Matt Bianco and Napalm Death on the way.

Sounds a strange mixture? That's the point. Presented by Craig Charles, it takes you on a roundabout ride through different genres, some you'll know and like, some you think you'll hate until you hear them.

What's That Noise? starts on Tuesday, 3 October, 4.35pm on BBC 1.

The Indy 28.9.89

Reviews

BATMAN IS HERE!
...and it's the biggest blockbuster this year

Cert 12. Warner Bros. Out Aug 11.

Who can catch the Caped Crusader? Who can jest with The Joker? As the comic book super-hero bursts onto our screens, Great Britain's already going bat barmy!

Batman has already smashed box office records in the US and you don't have to have a bat brain to see why.

The $35m movie's got an all-star cast that includes Michael 'Beetlejuice' Keaton as Batman, alias Bruce Wayne, Kim 'My Stepmother is an Alien' Basinger as his girlfriend Vicki Vale and best of all, wildman Jack Nicholson as the evil Joker.

The film is an extravagent adventure that's at least a million miles away from the tacky, light-hearted '60s TV version we all know and love.

The movie version sees a far more sinister, serious armour-plated Batman who's without his TV trusty sidekick, Robin. In fact you don't hear one "Holy smoke, Batman!" muttered or a ZAP! POW! BIFF! in the whole film. Missing also is the famous *"Da, na, na, na..."* theme.

Instead Batman gets a decent pair of tights, some steamy scenes with journo Vicki Vale, and a whole new set of hi-tech gadgets – you'll barely recognise the futuristic Batplane and Batmobile!

The plot is basically the good guys vs bad guys. The difference is that this Batman has a dark side. Sometimes you get the feeling he's just itching to say: "C'mon punk, make my day" and blow the baddies to kingdom come.

Interestingly, we also get a flashback which explains why he decided to wage war against the forces of evil. Basically it all goes back to when he was just nine-year-old Bruce Wayne who witnesses the brutal murder of his rich parents.

Jack Nicholson goes grinningly over-the-top as The Joker who wants to take over Gotham City and turn it into a gansters' paradise.

And like Sean Connery in *Indiana Jones and the Last Crusade*, his sheer class almost steals the show.

Michael Keaton is surprisingly good as the Caped Crusader while Kim Basinger gives a solid bimbo-like performance as Vicki Vale. But for my money (He didn't have to pay! – Ed) it's the way the film looks that's really impressive.

Creepy Gotham City looks like it's never seen a sunbeam and makes you wonder whether it's worth saving at all, while the special effects are just ace.

Oh, and I'm not surprised it didn't get a 'PG' Certificate, because they are some quite gory, violent scenes!

Batman's well worth queuing for (He **did** queue! – Ed), and shouldn't be missed. And although Indiana Jones may be more fun, Batman certainly packs a heavier punch! Zapp!

Scoop 10.8.89

THE BRITISH ARE COMING
written by Alan Gilby, directed by Pavel Douglas, presented by the Natural Theatre Company (Battersea Arts Centre)

Set slightly in the future this quasi-comedy concerns a British trade delegation to Siberia. Why it should be Siberia remains a mystery, except that it provides the excuse to have somebody dressed as what appears to be a beetroot with a hammer and sickle on its head. As the computer controlled exhibition centre starts to go wildly wrong members of the delegation die hideous deaths, mostly due to a very indifferent script, which flops about like a dying cod. Who done it? Maybe the lager-lout mechanic, who built the machine, can furnish the answer. He provides most of the few interesting moments in an otherwise uninspiring play that attempts to be both funny and to address serious topics simultaneously. Firing at practically any issue that moves, it ends up doing neither. The performers – Oliver Childs, Brian Popay and Ellen J Wilks – put up a heroic fight but the script defeats them, with a laboured over-written structure and jokes that you can see coming half a mile away through thick mist. Interestingly the only moment when it all suddenly springs to life is when they produce a very gutsy send up of Shakespeare. Alas, it is the only chance they get.
STEPHEN DINSDALE

City Limits 7.12.89

Letter writing

Aim To write letters to newspapers expressing personal opinions

Editors want to hear from you. They like to know what their readers are thinking. They know that the letters page is popular with their readers, who also want to know what other people are thinking.

It is an interesting challenge for you to try to get your opinions into print so that you can share them with a large number of readers. You will probably find it easier to get your letter into a young people's newspaper such as the *Early Times*, but you should also try the local paper and even some of the nationals.

First of all, learn to recognise the kinds of letters that newspapers print. Different papers will have different policies about the kinds of topics they want to publish. You can learn from the letters that you need to be familiar with the issues the paper is covering, you need to be concise, you need to get straight to the point, you need to be topical and if possible express a fresh or unusual point of view.

Advice from an editor
- Always sign your letter.
- Make sure your writing is legible. Type the letter if possible, using double spacing.
- Write something that is likely to appeal to the kinds of readers the paper attracts.
- Be honest.
- Make the most of your youth, expressing a 'young person's angle' on the topic you are writing about. A child's view on discipline in the home, for instance, would attract an editor.
- Make sure your spelling and punctuation are accurate.
- Once you have written, try again and do not be disappointed if it takes some time to get into print.

Letter writing

Study the readers' letters printed below.

- Discuss in small groups what reasons they give for their opinions. How convincing do you find them?
- If you had space for only two of these letters in your paper, which ones would you choose, and why?

Fair games?

WHY ARE games and PE compulsory? It's a nightmare - we are forced screaming and kicking to participate, come rain, shine or fifteen feet of snow.

We are made to run a circuit five times. Then, as if that wasn't enough, we have to play hockey, netball, or high jump. Being only five foot tall, this isn't always the easiest thing to do.

To top it all, our sports teacher is horrible. She loves watching us struggle and wince at the impossible sporting feats ahead of us.

Why, oh why, must games be compulsory?

Elli Kater, 12

The Indy 12.10.89

I FEEL VERY strongly about the damage being done to the ozone layer by CFC's. Why doesn't the Government ban all aerosols now?

They keep saying 'steps are being taken', but we need something more forceful to make more people take positive action. Regarding aerosols, it's not as if there are no benefits to the individual using non-aerosol products - for example, non-aerosol hairspray lasts about two or three times longer than the aerosol, and so in the long run is a lot cheaper.

I also think that lead-free petrol should be law for vehicles from 1990, and not from the proposed year 2000. It seems that the Government's current motto is 'why do today what you can put off till tomorrow?'. Not everyone is going to spend time and money doing something unless it becomes law.

J Mason

Grapevine 10.4.89

I'M SURE I speak for the majority of Britain when I say that the new format for 'Top of the Pops' is absolute drivel. How you're supposed to enjoy a song cut to two or three minutes is beyond me. I thought it was quality and not quantity that matters, but obviously I'm wrong.

L. Barnes

Grapevine 10.4.89

Racist Britain

I AM writing to complain about racism. I cannot see any difference between coloured people and white people, except the difference in the colour of their skin.

You only need to switch on the television on a Saturday night for blatant examples of racism. I don't know why people have to mock different races for a laugh. The world would be a very boring place if we all looked the same.

And sexism is no better than racism. The Church of England is trying to stop women from being priests at the moment. Men and women were supposed to be created equal, but some people obviously still think that men are superior. It is just not right.

Nowadays people can't open their mouths half the time without being racist or sexist.

Cooking, cleaning, washing and ironing are supposed to be women's work, but I can do these things, and I am not a woman. Men are supposed to handle money and go out to work, but that's not necessarily true either. My dad may work, but my mum works as well. My mum also handles all the money she earns.

Graeme Mathieson, 10

The Indy 30.11.89

Write a letter to a newspaper, one of the other group newspapers, for instance, expressing your opinions about any topical issue and giving reasons for your opinions. Keep any letters you receive for your group newspaper.

TASK 5 The Problem Page

Aim To work in a group and produce a problem page of readers' letters and the expert's replies

The problem pages in newspapers and magazines are much scorned, often parodied but nevertheless very popular, especially among young readers.

They fulfil the need of having someone to talk to. Often people cannot talk to those closest to them because they are part of the problem. Newspapers can provide an objective, unemotional setting for the problem to be aired.

Most newspapers print the letter, often in shortened form, followed by the expert's comments, with suggestions about where further advice can be obtained.

Here is an example of a problem page letter from *The Indy*. Discuss whether or not the writer was serious and whether that matters.

A Comic Idol

THIS PROBLEM will probably sound very silly. But I don't know what to do. I am completely and totally and utterly in love with Ben Elton.

I have pictures of him all over my walls. And I can't think or talk about anyone else. Sometimes I think that if he met me, he would fall in love with me too. I build up these dreams in my head. And I'm only happy when I think about us together.

I imagine our conversations. And I imagine him thinking I was really intelligent and witty too.

Sometimes it makes me so frustrated I want to cry. And I do cry. But everybody tells me to shut up and stop being so stupid. What am I to do? I am so unhappy.

Maria, 11, Hull

The Indy 26.10.89

Write a reply to the letter as if you were the 'agony aunt'.

 In your groups, write at least five problem letters and send them to other groups to use in their group newspapers. Keep the letters you receive and write responses to them for your paper.

Comparing story openings

Aim To understand how journalists can distort information by the way they report it

The two stories on Sheet 44 were based on the same information – a survey by the Health Education Authority about teenage behaviour.

Every newspaper receives a copy of this survey and decides whether or not to assign a reporter to write about its findings. In this case the *Daily Express* writer is Colin Bell and the *Independent* writer is the education editor, Peter Wilby. Each journalist has selected different bits of the report to emphasise and has chosen words which show his own attitudes to teenagers. The resulting stories give two different versions of the same survey.

As a reader it is important to realise that a writer's own opinions influence the information you are given.

Compare the two story openings to see how they give different versions of the same material.

- Which headline is more critical of teenagers? How?
- Which opening paragraph gives a more positive view of teenagers?
- In one particular detail the two lead paragraphs contradict each other. What is it?
- Read carefully through the two extracts and say what teenage behaviour they agree on, what they disagree about, and what one mentions but the other does not.
- With reference to the extracts, talk about the ways in which bias depends on:
    Use of certain words and phrases
    Selecting/missing out certain information.

Comparing story openings

Layabout lifestyle of the teenage tipplers

By COLIN BELL

TODAY'S teenagers spend much of their lives drinking, smoking and lounging about watching TV, according to a new survey.

Many start dabbling in sex as children but they are not keen on homework and would not dream of reading a book just for the fun of it.

Half of them hold down regular jobs, like paper rounds and baby sitting, but do not save their wages.

Most of the cash—on average £10 a week—goes on records, discos, clothes and bus fares.

The study into the teenage lifestyle is published by the Health Education Authority which quizzed more than 18,000 pupils at 88 schools in England, Scotland, Wales, and Northern Ireland.

Daily Express 6.11.87

Typical teenager is TV addict, survey finds

By Peter Wilby
Education Editor

THE TYPICAL British teenager is a clean, hardworking non-smoker, who spends generously on presents but is somewhat prone to headaches and ill-at-ease with the opposite sex, according to research published yesterday.

The teenage day starts with cereal, a glance at a popular newspaper and possibly a morning paper-round. It continues with regular attention to teeth and smelly armpits but an excessive intake of alcohol, sugar and fat; winds down with the minimum of homework and reading, and lots of goggling at television; and concludes with a bedtime between 10 and 11pm, after abortive attempts to extract information about sex from parents.

This picture emerges from a survey of 18,000 adolescents, who were questioned on a school day during term-time.

The Independent 6.11.87

Interpreting a survey

Aim To write different reports based on the same information

Here are some conclusions about the teaching of maths in primary schools from a report by the HMI. The conclusions have been adapted slightly. The report is called 'Aspects of Primary Education: the Teaching and Learning of Mathematics'.

Work either in pairs or as two halves of a class to reproduce two reports of the same information. One report should be very positive about the teachers' achievements in very difficult circumstances. The other should be critical of teachers and the system. Exchange and read each others' reports.

You can select from the information and include your own opinions.

 Save your reports for your group newspaper.

- Maths work in primary schools is too often limited to boring pencil and paper exercises done from badly produced work cards.
- Some good schools encourage practical problem-solving related to children's daily lives.
- Teachers in primary schools are not given enough time for lesson preparation.
- Hardly any primary teachers have higher qualifications in maths.
- Many teachers have to deal with classes that are too big.
- Most schools give high priority to maths and teach it for the equivalent of one day per week.
- Arithmetic is given a lot of attention in all schools.
- Half of the schools surveyed had good results in arithmetic.
- In 25% of schools performance in maths was judged to be poor.
- 30% of the rest were judged to be good in some aspects.
- Schools rely too much on commercially produced maths schemes.
- Fewer than 4% of teachers had a main qualification in maths.
- There were 70 good schools in the survey and in these schools the inspectors found:
  pupils learned tables
  they knew how to use calculators
  they worked together in groups and discussed maths problems
  work was set at different levels of ability but the basic stimulus was common to all
  children found problems set were relevant to their daily lives.

TASK 3 Comparing two interpretations

Aim To analyse and compare two news stories about the same event and to identify bias

Look at the stories *Pupils play to learn* and *Dodging lessons* on Sheets 47 and 48.

- Describe what you see in the pictures. Are the pictures giving any messages about the activity? Which one makes the activity look more purposeful?

- Each caption includes a pun. Explain the meaning of the puns and say whether they give a favourable or an unfavourable impression about what is going on.

- Compare the headlines. Do they tell you anything about the writers' opinions about what is happening?

- Which article includes more interviews? How does this help you to get a clearer picture of what is going on?

- Compare the information in the two stories. Are there any differences between the two?

- Make a list of the opinions stated or implied by the writers. Which writer is more critical of what is going on?

FOOTNOTE: A Butlin's spokesperson said that there is no holiday camp at Brighton, but that there is a holiday hotel there. He thought it unlikely that the *Daily Mail* reporter had attended one of the educational courses. Does this make any difference to your reaction to the two stories?

▶ Comparing two interpretations

Pupils play to learn at Butlin's

By Simon Midgley
Education Reporter

MORE THAN 500 pupils are playing snooker, darts and fruit machines at a Butlin's holiday camp to prepare for the new GCSE examination.

The pioneering educational experiment of running six-day residential courses at Somerwest World, Minehead, has received a mixed reaction from teachers.

While the pupils appeared to be having a whale of a time gaining practical experience of probability theory, statistics and angles of deflection from playing games, there were problems on the £69-plus-Vat courses, which are paid for by parents.

Teachers complained about the standard camper's food — chips with everything — the accommodation, poor course planning, equipment shortages and inappropriately or under-qualified support staff.

The idea was that 530 14- to 16-year-olds and 50 teachers from 18 comprehensive schools in Kent, Oxfordshire, Essex, Walsall, Bristol and Hampshire spend six days away from home studying maths, science, English, art, drama and the humanities using the 169-acre camp's extensive facilities — theatres, sports facilities, video cameras, photographic services — and examining the history, flora and fauna of the surrounding hills of Exmoor, the nearby beaches and the ancient settlements behind Porlock.

As it happens, an 11,000-bed out-of-season holiday camp is a slightly incongruous place for a schools trip. Apart from the acres of advertising hoardings for Skol Coca-Cola and Rothmans cigarettes there is something rather desolate about acres of shuttered bars and restaurants, the relentless jollity of the ubiquitous plaster clowns and the fact that the kiddies' fun pool has been colonised by wintering ducks.

But this was the least of some

Fruits of learning: Pupils working on a maths project at Butlin's.

teachers' worries. In the jungle-like gloom of the Beachcomber's bar, complete with waterfall, fetid grottoes and bamboo furniture, Debbie Stephens, a drama and English teacher from The Ashcombe School in Dorking, is supervising a mime class. She complains: "My colleague and I have made complaint after complaint after complaint."

She has brought 24 children to study geography, media studies and drama. At first she says the children were put into damp old chalets on the periphery of the camp where the beds were wet and cold. "They stank to high heaven," she said. Her school and another complained and they were promptly moved to better accommodation. Her problems, however, continued.

The media studies work was hampered by video camera shortages and faulty equipment. After protests, more cameras were found but one had a flat battery

and the two studio cameras failed to play back so the children were unable to see their work. "If the equipment is not working or not available, we might as well not bother," she said.

Her other complaints — about shortages of teaching materials, poor planning, over-large teaching groups and insufficient support staff were echoed by four teachers from Meopham High School, near Maidstone. They were also under the impression that specialist advisers would teach the children giving them a chance to assess the children.

Sonia Delay, head of third year, said: "The idea is very good. But there is a lot of scope for improvement in orgnisation . . . subjects, domestic arrangements and food." Other teachers, however, were clearly satisfied. Peter Gain, mathematics adviser for Hampshire who is helping 14-year-old Lisa Davidson from Regent's Park school in Southampton

"conduct a mathematical investigation into probability" by making a tally of the symbols on a fruit machine, said he was pleased with the generous staff/pupil ratios and the opportunity to use equipment not found in schools for extended leisurely instruction.

Lisa agreed. "It is more of a reaxed atmosphere. We seem to learn more because there are more resources."

Wendy Bloxham, a drama teacher from Hayes Manor School in Middlesex, is supervising a group of 15 and 16-year-olds designing and making sets in the camp's main theatre where the huge stage, bigger than that at the Palladium, is more usually graced by the likes of Rod Hull or Jimmy Tarbuck.

"I would like to see a lot more of this," she said. "The children have much more individual attention than they would have in classes in school. They have the benefit of a whole day without being interrupted by bells and registration. We have not got the resources, equipment and expertise at our school. We wanted to take advantage of the theatrical experts and get hands on experience of the equipment."

Geoffrey Stone, head of the Rank Organisation's educational division, which runs the course, admits that there have been teething problems. There have been shortages of some basic materials — modelling clay, paper, theatrical make-up. The main problem as he sees it, however, is one of communication.

"To some extent we have not communicated as well as we might have done — that teachers come and teachers teach. What we provide is the resources in terms of buildings, equipment, senior advisory and academic people, support staff and study material in advance," he said.

Today the educational experiment continues when a fresh batch of schools descend on Butlin's for a week of Hi-de-Hi style schooling.

The Independent 9.11.87

Comparing two interpretations

Dodging lessons at the Hi-de-hi school

Darts and arithmetic ... but does it add up to education?

UNDER the familiar and fatuous motto 'learning can be fun' 500 pupils from 14 state schools have been spending six days at Butlin's Somerwest World, a holiday camp at Brighton.

The children, all aged 14 and 15, are studying for their General Certificate of Secondary Education. They are being 'continually assessed', not examined, it goes without saying.

By playing snooker in the camp's snooker hall they are supposed to learn about angles of deflection. By playing darts they are supposed to teach themselves addition and subtraction.

Tomfoolery

Fruit machines, adapted to work without money, are supposed to teach them about the laws of probability governing the winning of a jackpot.

In the evenings they enjoy the attractions of Waterworld and the Somerwest recreational facilities — and all at just over half the peak season cost.

Rank Educational Services run the course, under the direction of Mr Alan Ridgway, who in the holiday season is the camp's director of entertainments.

Full marks to him and to Butlins for their private enterprise filling their camp in off-season times with six-day 'field courses' for children.

No marks at all for the local education authorities who waste public funds on such tomfoolery.

No marks for the teachers who go along with it, preferring to play snooker, darts and fruit machines instead of teaching geometry, arithmetic and probability the hard and proper way.

No marks to the parents who encourage their children to think that learning is a matter of fun and not a matter of work.

Daily Mail 6.11.87

 Photojournalism

Aim To study a selection of photographs and discuss the messages they convey

Photographs in a newspaper usually illustrate or emphasise the main point of a story. Sometimes they can be more important than the story, so that the words are used to 'illustrate' the picture.

Imagine that the photographs here and on the following Sheets have been entered for a 'News Picture of the Year' competition.

In pairs or small groups discuss what each picture is 'saying' about human behaviour. Then discuss the quality of the picture in terms of its clarity and composition. Which pictures do you reject? Why? Decide on the best picture and give reasons for your choice. Tell other groups about your choice and reasons.

A

▶ **Photojournalism**

B

C

D

Photojournalism

E

F

G

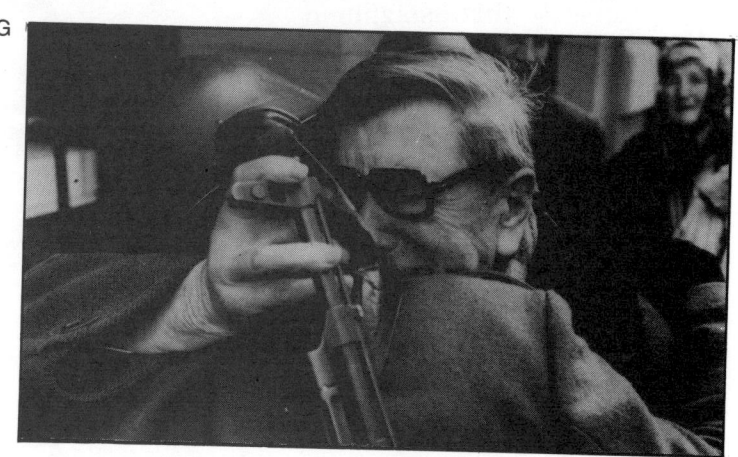

© John Price, 1991. *Newspapers*, Macmillan English.
Copyright restrictions on page ii.

TASK
2 The caption as interpreter

Aim To understand how captions can alter the messages which photographs convey

On Sheet 53 are two pictures of the same incident. On Thursday, 25 November 1988, students demonstrated near the Houses of Parliament against government proposals to introduce loans instead of grants for higher education.

The police stopped the students from getting close to the Houses of Parliament because demonstrations within a mile of Westminster are banned when Parliament is sitting.

Although the two pictures of the police and students are similar, the captions give different interpretations of what is going on.

- Which words in the *Guardian* caption show that it is more critical of the police?
- Which words in the *Sun* caption show that it is more critical of the students?
- Write a new caption which is neutral, criticising neither police nor students.

Write two captions for the picture shown here that suggest first that the policeman is a guardian or protector of people and property and second that he is in some sort of danger.

Choose one or more pictures from those in this assignment, depending on how much time you have, and work in pairs to speculate on possible stories that they could be illustrating.

Write a caption, a headline and a 100-word story in newspaper style for each picture. Keep the work for your group newspaper.

The caption as interpreter

The Sun 25.11.88

FLASHPOINT . . . howling students flee as mounted cops charge the rioting mob during clashes

The Guardian 25.11.88

Police and demonstrators clash south of Westminster Bridge after officers charged students who had broken away from a rally nearby

Cartoons

Aim To understand how cartoons are used in newspapers to communicate ideas, information and opinion on topical issues

Newspapers use cartoons to illustrate and comment on topical issues. A cartoonist's job is to use humour to entertain, inform and influence the reader.

The cartoon below is by Cummings and appeared in the *Daily Express* during the summer holidays of 1989. It is typical of the kinds of general interest cartoons that the national tabloids carry.

Daily Express 4.8.89

There had been a series of stories in the popular press about 'holiday disasters' in Southern European resorts. Fire had been raging across the South of France, British holidaymakers had caught typhoid while in Spain, a gang of drunken British youths had murdered a Spanish waiter and raw sewage had somehow got into a swimming pool at a popular resort. An air traffic controllers' strike in France meant that holidaymakers had had long waits at airports. Meanwhile back in Britain there had been an unusual heatwave and there was a certain amount of gloating about people who were 'suffering' on their foreign holidays.

Cartoons

- What joke is Cummings making about Mediterranean holidays?
- Why is the brochure so large?
- How is it different from a normal brochure?

Because cartoonists have to draw people who are easily recognisable as types, they have to oversimplify and use standard images. You know a man is rich, for example, because he smokes a big cigar. Teachers in some cartoons still wear gowns and mortar boards and carry canes. So cartoons often contain several messages. Look at the Cummings cartoon again.

- How can you recognise who is a) the judge, b) the members of the legal profession, c) the police, d) the jury, and e) the criminal?
- Are there any dangers as well as advantages in this kind of visual shorthand?
  In particular discuss the way the criminal looks and is dressed.

Now analyse this Giles cartoon for all its possible meanings. What does it tell you about a) school buildings, b) pupils, c) teachers? How 'true to life' is it?

Daily Express 17.11.88

"How many times must I tell you: 'Is not Noddy the most stupid. . .you ever saw? 'NOT 'Aint Noddy the most stupid . . . you ever saw?'"

Cartoons

Here are two cartoons about serious subjects: animal rights and food contamination. Discuss how the cartoonists are using exaggeration to make something appear ridiculous. Try this technique yourself with any topical issue or one of the following: pollution, fashion, equal opportunities, new technology, fast food.

Scoop 10·8·89

from *Earth Mirth*

Graphics

Aim To examine how drawings and charts can be used in news reporting to convey information

Large parts of most newspapers are devoted to providing readers with simple information. There are sports results, team lists, league tables, weather reports, race cards, what's on lists, share prices, radio and television schedules and so on. Newspapers tackle the problem of conveying information clearly and concisely in a number of ways.

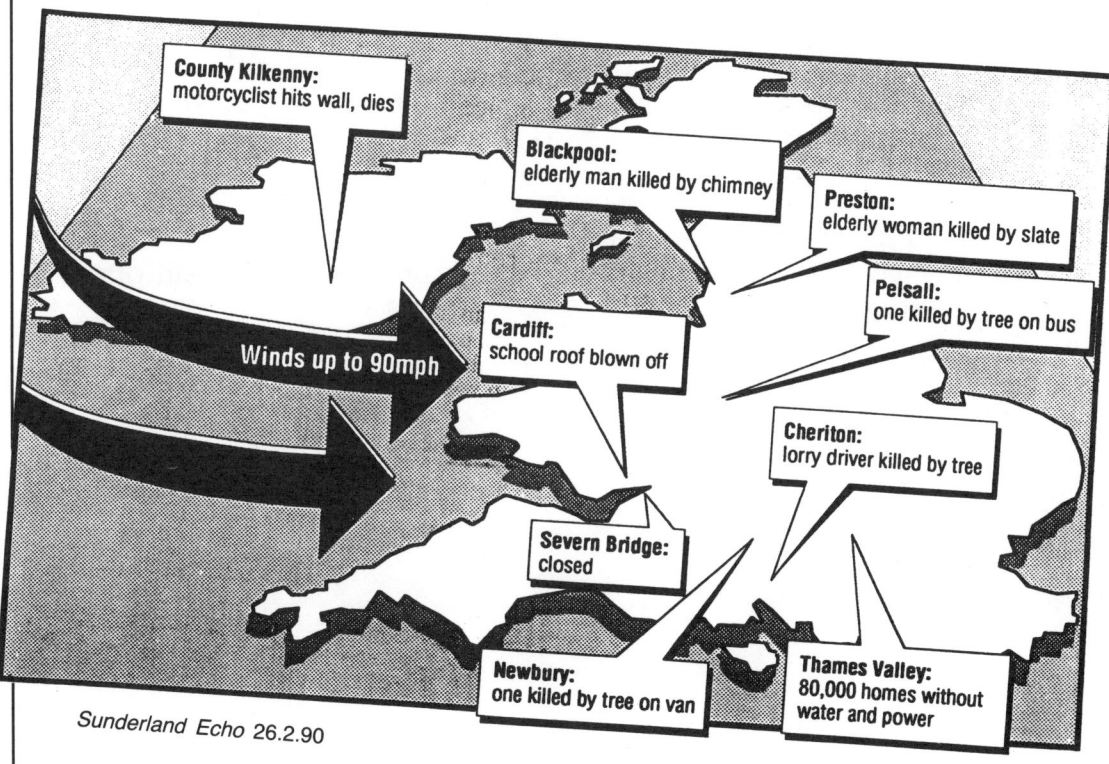

Sunderland Echo 26.2.90

Write an accompanying 150-word news story about the damage caused by the stormy weather.

Graphics

Here is another graphic illustrating the income and expenditure involved in running the Commonwealth Games

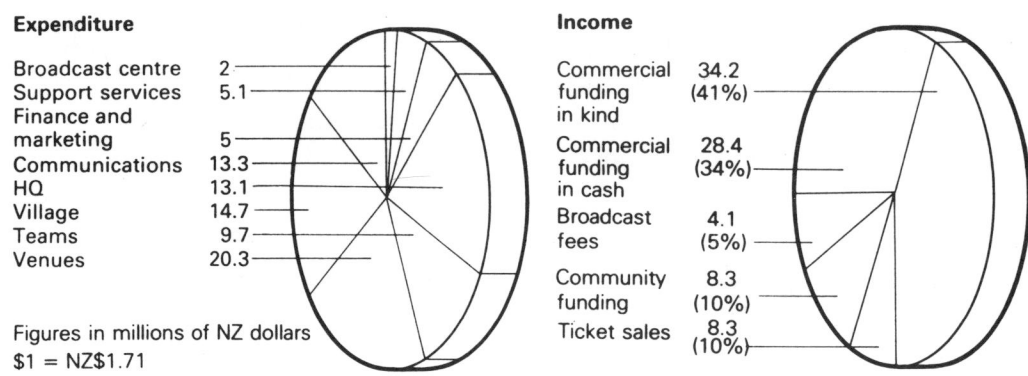

Expenditure

Broadcast centre	2
Support services	5.1
Finance and marketing	5
Communications	13.3
HQ	13.1
Village	14.7
Teams	9.7
Venues	20.3

Figures in millions of NZ dollars
$1 = NZ$1.71

Income

Commercial funding in kind	34.2	(41%)
Commercial funding in cash	28.4	(34%)
Broadcast fees	4.1	(5%)
Community funding	8.3	(10%)
Ticket sales	8.3	(10%)

Write an article based on the information in the graphic and then discuss what is lost and gained by using only words instead of words and pictures.

 Design a graphic to illustrate any aspect of the Richard Branson story on page 15. Keep your work for your group newspaper.

5 Breaking up text

Aim To understand how the way text is laid out on a page can make it easier to understand

If a newspaper has to report a large amount of information it will sometimes list the main points rather than have a large body of text. Sheet 60 contains an extract from *The Independent* about social trends in the British Isles. Notice how the information has been made easier to understand by the writer picking out the main points on a regional bases. Readers not interested in the whole report can easily pick out the regions that they are particularly interested in. The main points for each region are highlighted and written in note form as lists.

So that you can see the difference made by reducing information to note form, rewrite the information for your own region in full sentences as one long paragraph.

▶ Breaking up text

SCOTLAND

- ☐ Most likely to read a Sunday paper.
- ☐ Lowest proportion of ethnic minorities.
- ☐ Largest proportion of drink-drive prosecutions.
- ☐ Largest proportion spent on alcohol and tobacco.
- ☐ Population fell by 1.3 per cent between 1981 and 1987 to 5.1 million.
- ☐ Lowest pupil-teacher ratios.
- ☐ Crime up 19 per cent 1987 over 1981.
- ☐ Unemployment 11.2 per cent in 1988
- ☐ Worst increase in drug offences 1981-87, with a near tripling in the number of drug offences.

WALES

- ☐ Lowest rate of robbery.
- ☐ People most likely to have long-standing illness.
- ☐ With Northern Ireland, the highest crime clear-up rate.
- ☐ Highest average numbers of days lost through strikes (1978-87)
- ☐ Highest proportion spent on food.
- ☐ Crime up 37 per cent 1981-87
- ☐ Average male earnings £218 a week, lower than anywhere in England and Scotland.

NORTHERN IRELAND

- ☐ Lowest rate of drug offences.
- ☐ Most spent per head on pollution control.
- ☐ Highest rate of still births
- ☐ Highest proportion of speeding offences in 1987.
- ☐ Highest unemployment (16.4 per cent). Double the average.
- ☐ Lowest average male earnings (£215 a week 1988).
- ☐ Lower proportion than any region spent on housing.
- ☐ Lowest proportion of pensioners.
- ☐ Highest average household size of 3.07 people.

EAST ANGLIA

- ☐ Highest rate of private sector housebuilding.
- ☐ Fastest growing population — 1 per cent a year.
- ☐ Most sparsely-populated region in England
- ☐ Lowest crime rate in England and Wales.
- ☐ Lowest unemployment (4.8 per cent).
- ☐ Lowest day-loss rate through strikes (1978-87).
- ☐ Second lowest proportion of children born outside marriage in the UK
- ☐ Highest household expenditure on leisure goods and services and lowest on alcohol and tobacco.
- ☐ Lowest infant mortality rate — 7.8 per 1,000.

SOUTH-EAST

- ☐ Worst crime clear-up rate.
- ☐ Home for half Britain's ethnic minorities.
- ☐ Highest male average earnings (£283 a week 1988).
- ☐ Only area to spend more on housing than food.
- ☐ Eat most fruit.
- ☐ Most likely to have a dishwasher, telephone or video, but least likely to have a washing machine.
- ☐ Has 30 per cent of total UK population and is second most densely populated region after the North-west.
- ☐ Highest proportion of 16-year-olds staying on in education.

NORTH

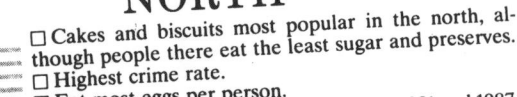

- ☐ Cakes and biscuits most popular in the north, although people there eat the least sugar and preserves.
- ☐ Highest crime rate.
- ☐ Eat most eggs per person.
- ☐ Population fell by 1.3 per cent between 1981 and 1987.
- ☐ Cheapest homes. In 1987 average house price of £27,300.
- ☐ Lowest participation rate in further education.

YORKSHIRE AND HUMBERSIDE

- ☐ Eat most fish and least cheese.
- ☐ Highest infant mortality rate
- ☐ Best yields for wheat, barley and oats in 1987.
- ☐ Second highest rates in England and Wales of violence against the person and sexual offences.
- ☐ Population fell by 0.4 per cent 1981-1987.
- ☐ Average household expenditure of £157 a week in 1986, with only people in the North spending less.

EAST MIDLANDS

- ☐ Highest rates of violent crime and sexual offences.
- ☐ Drink the most milk.
- ☐ Lowest average women's wages (£145 a week on average 1988).
- ☐ Second highest percentage (69 per cent) of owner-occupied dwellings.
- ☐ More homes with central heating than anywhere els (77%).

WEST MIDLANDS

- ☐ Highest proportion of ethnic minority groups in pr vate households — 7.7 per cent in period 1985-1987.
- ☐ Highest proportion of males.
- ☐ Least likely to have central heating.
- ☐ Ownership of all consumer durables lower than t average for 1985-6.
- ☐ Eat most meat.
- ☐ Crime up 40 per cent between 1981 and 1987.

NORTH-WEST

- ☐ Highest proportion of births outside marriage.
- ☐ Highest crime rate 1987.
- ☐ Lowest weekly average household expenditure.
- ☐ Women's wages higher than anywhere except south-east (£153 per week).
- ☐ Highest ownership of colour televisions.
- ☐ Lowest rate for fatal or serious car accidents.
- ☐ Most densely-populated region

SOUTH-WEST

- ☐ Highest car ownership — 373 per 1,000 people.
- ☐ Eat more of most vegetables.
- ☐ Highest proportion of pensioners.
- ☐ School-leavers most likely to have no qualificat
- ☐ Most self-employed (14.2 per cent).
- ☐ Lowest average household size — 2.58 persons
- ☐ Highest rate of fatal or serious road casualties per 100,000.

The Independen

Display advertisements

Aim To study and apply the techniques used in display advertising in newspapers

Display advertisements are much larger than classified advertisements and can appear anywhere in the paper. They advertise large organisations and businesses.

Display advertisements are often prepared by professional advertising agencies. They contain, usually, a visual message, a slogan or headline, selling points and an action line.

Look at the advertisement for Save the Children and discuss how effective are the choice of picture and the headline.

- What, if anything, is the advertisement 'selling'?
- How is it trying to persuade readers to give money?
- Which part of the advertisement (the 'action line') tries to get the reader to do something?

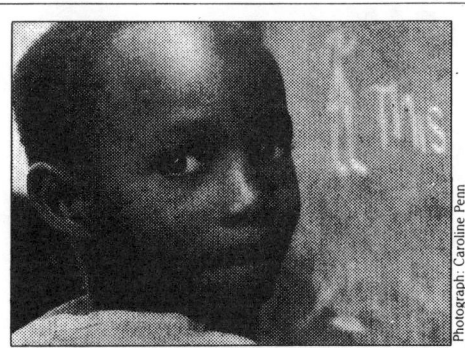

Photograph: Caroline Penn

Open the school doors for Lamin

Lamin's teachers know how bright he is; they know he's earned his place in secondary school.

Yet because Lamin's family can't afford his fees, the school doors may soon shut on him…

… <u>unless you can help</u>.

Just £2.36 a week will ensure Lamin takes his place at school and enjoys the education he's worked so hard for.

There are 100 other children like Lamin in Gambia, Lesotho, Uganda and Swaziland. Just as bright and just as desperate to find sponsors.

Please fill out the coupon, and help to give these bright children the future they deserve.

Yes I wish to sponsor a child at £120 per annum and enclose my first annual payment. ☐

I would like more information about the scheme and details of how I can pay by instalments.   (Please tick appropriate box) ☐

I am unable to sponsor a child, please accept my donation of £ _____

Signature _____

Name Mr/Mrs/Miss/Ms _____
(BLOCK CAPITALS PLEASE)
Address _____

_____ Postcode _____

Return to: Sponsorship Controller, Dept 9020113, FREEPOST, Save the Children, (Registered Charity no. 213890), 17 Grove Lane, London SE5 8BR. Or ring on 01-703 5400 for further information

Save the Children

Display advertisements

Compare these two advertisements for activity holidays. Talk about the headlines, the selling points, the clarity of layout and the action lines. Which one does the better job?

Design your own advertisement using this picture. Invent the name of an acivity holiday company, think up a slogan or headline, choose about five selling points and include an action line. Keep the advertisement for your group newspaper.

TASK

2 **Classified advertisements**

Aim To practise writing classified advertisements for newspapers

Most newspapers have a section called 'classified' advertising. This section is used by individuals and small businesses to let readers know what is for sale. 'Classified' means that the advertisements are grouped under different headings, so that readers can quickly find what they want to buy.

Classified adverts are charged according to the number of words used, or the space, measured in column centimetres, which is used. It pays, therefore, to get your message across in as few words as possible. A kind of classified shorthand has developed, where there are no complete sentences and standard abbreviations such as o.n.o. – or nearest offer – are common.

Re-write these three adverts in complete sentences without abbreviations:

Corner bath with taps. Pop-up plug, spray, complete installation kit, cream. In ex. cond. £110 o.n.o.

Suzuki Tsi 85. Low mlge. MOT. Spare tyre. 12,000 mls. v.g.c. £250.

L. Vict./Edw sideboard. £100 o.n.o. Old chest drawers £15. Also other items.

The following advert is working out rather expensive! Shorten it so that it still makes sense, but costs as little as possible.

'I have decided to sell a present which somebody gave me but I do not really want. It is a TOPNOTCH microcomputer, which has hardly been used. There are a few games to go with it and there is a RITEUP printer as well. I would like £250 for the lot, but I would be prepared to accept something less than that. If you are interested why don't you telephone me at home? My telephone number is 9173460 and I am usually home soon after the end of school.'

Writing a press release

Aim To understand the purpose and structure of a press release and to write your own press release.

Organisations which want publicity often employ specialist writers to prepare press releases.

The purpose of a press release is to give information to newspapers, television and radio. A good press release is written in a journalistic style, so that it can be easily used by newspaper and magazine editors in their publications.

Here is an example of a press release:

Newtown Comprehensive School

Forrester Road, Newtown, Middleshire MN15 1BX Tel: 087 417635

Headteacher: Mrs Joan Appleby BA, MEd.

Press Release
Release date: immediate

PUPILS STAY SILENT TO AID THE STARVING

Pupils at Newtown School are to spend a morning in complete silence as a way of helping the victims of the famine in Africa.

The sponsored silence, brainchild of 16-year-old pupil, Gavin Fairchild, will raise over £1000, which will be given to Oxfam to pay for emergency food supplies for the famine victims of North Africa.

Headmistress, Joan Appleby said, 'The idea was suggested by Gavin after his Practical RE group discussed ways of helping people in trouble. I thought it was an excellent idea and gave it my full support.'

The 1100 pupils in the school aim to go through a whole morning's lessons in complete silence.

'It will be a big challenge,' said Gavin 'and I think that some people will not make it, but even if the scheme is only 75% successful, we should have enough money to save hundreds of lives.'

The project is only one of many ideas that the Practical RE group has organised. They recently spent a day helping disabled people to do their shopping at a local supermarket and they have helped to re-build a children's play area destroyed by vandals.

Further information from the headteacher at the school.

End.

Writing a press release

A good press release should have the following characteristics:

1 A clear indication of the organisation's name and address
2 A release date to show when the information is news
3 A heading or headline
4 Short paragraphs
5 Quotations from people involved in the story
6 A newspaper style
7 The name of a contact from whom extra information can be obtained if necessary
8 Succinct information in no more than 250 words
9 The main point of the story in the first paragraph
10 The full names of the people involved in the story, with ages where appropriate.

Look again at the press release on Sheet 64. Does it have these ten characteristics?

Write a press release for a forthcoming event in your school.

● You will need to check that your information is accurate by talking to someone responsible for organising the event.

● Try to interview people involved and get brief quotations from them.

● Send the press releases to the news editors of your local newspaper and you might just have the story published!

● Do not expect a reply, however, as news editors do not have time to reply to press releases.

 Write an article based on the 'Pupils Stay Silent' press release for your newspaper.

2 Re-working a press release

Aim To write a news report based on a press release

Reporters usually select information from press releases that are too long. They have to pick out what they think are the main points of the story that will interest their readers.

Look at the Livewire press release below and write a 100-word story for a teenage newspaper that sells to young people in the town of Sunderland. You can keep to the original text as much as you want, but you must have exactly 100 words in the story. Think up a new headline of no more than five words.

YOUNG·IDEAS·AT·WORK

<u>YOUNG INVENTOR AIMS FOR RECORD BUSINESS PRIZE</u>

A young Wearside vegetarian food manufacturer who has invented a unique soya cheese is in the running for a record share of £5250 worth of prizes for bright business ideas.

Richard Friend, 24, who operates the Claremont Cheese Company from 2 Claremont Terrace, Sunderland, is one of 35 young people aged between 16 and 25 who have so far entered this year's Livewire Competition, designed to encourage new business initiatives by young people. The competition is sponsored nationally by Shell UK with substantial local support from the Northern Rock Building Society, the City Action Team and Borough Councils.

The former Biology graduate's inspiration to start up his business came following an academic project he undertook while at Sunderland Polytechnic.

more...

© John Price, 1991. Newspapers, Macmillan English.
Copyright restrictions on page ii.

Re-working a press release

'I was specifically looking for a worthwhile project which could be useful to both myself and the community when I hit upon the idea of producing soya dairy produce', said Richard.

If he is successful in the Livewire County Final, to be judged in April, he will receive £1500 cash prize, and will then compete at regional level. He could also go on to the UK Finals to be held in London in June which carries a top prize of £3000.

As part of the scheme, a group of experts from local industry and commerce have been recruited to act as advisers passing on business advice to the young entrants. Richard has been paired with Vince Wright, General Manager of the Sunderland Youth Enterprise Centre who meets the young food manufacturer at intervals to advise on his business strategy.

Anyone interested in starting their own business are urged to enter Livewire now. Entry leaflets are available from Livewire, Freepost, Newcastle Upon Tyne, NE1 1BR. Closing date for entries is 31 January 1988.

- END -

CONTACT

Gary Nagel
Newcastle Youth Enterprise Centre
25 Low Friar Street
Newcastle Upon Tyne
NE1 5UE
Tel. (091) 2616009 - work
      (091) 4105413 - home

LIVEWIRE UK OFFICE
60 GRAINGER STREET · NEWCASTLE UPON TYNE NE1 5JG · TELEPHONE 091-261 5584

FOOTNOTE Although the closing date for the competition was in 1988, Livewire continues to offer support for young people wishing to set up their own business.

TASK

1 **Pagination**

Aim To decide on the number and size of pages for your newspaper and on the content of each page

The realistic choices for your page size are A4 (the size of this page) or A3, about the size of a tabloid paper.

The process of making a newspaper involves planning, writing, checking, selecting, printing and distribution.

 If you have worked through this course and stored your work, you should have almost completed the writing and you should have done some planning.

You will now need to decide how to put your pages together, whether you want to staple them or fold them, for instance.

If you have some money you can ask a professional printer to help with anything from typesetting and printing, which is expensive, to simpler jobs like collating, folding and stapling.

If you are working with a word processor, it is worth knowing that some printers are willing to handle text that has been stored on disk and this cuts down the printing costs considerably.

When you have decided how many pages you want, draw up a master plan like the one for an eight-page publication shown overleaf.

▶ Pagination

Make a list of each page's contents on your master plan.

p1

p2	p3

p4	p5

p6	p7	p8

2 Editorial selection

Aim To select and check the items for each page and then to publish your newspaper

- Collect all the work you have done during this course.

  You should have the following (numbers refer to Assignments):

  A masthead (1)
  Page designs (2)
  News stories based on interviews (2)
  Re-telling of a traditional story (3)
  A feature: interviews on a controversial subject (4)
  A report on 'The Rescue' (4)
  Personalised stories (4)
  A special feature (5)
  An editorial (6)
  Reviews (6)
  Letters (6)
  Problem letters (6)
  A report on a survey (7)
  Photographs (8)
  Cartoons (8)
  Graphics (8)
  Advertisements (9)
  Press release articles (10)

- In small groups, discuss the material you have available, choose the ones that will most appeal to your audience and allocate space on your master plans.

- Proof read all the articles you select, making sure there are no spelling mistakes and that the punctuation is accurate.

- Prepare everything except your front page. Make sure everything is typed or printed from your word processor. Cut and paste stories and pictures onto blank master grids the actual size of your publication.

- The front page should be completed on the day of publication. Fill it with news stories taken from the actual news of the day. Do re-writes of stories taken from newspapers or television. Make up your own headlines.

- Distribute your paper quickly so that it is fresh. Ask for feedback from anyone who reads it and then start planning for your next paper. Tell Rupert Murdoch to watch out!

PROCESS

Literacy
Skimming, scanning and
close reading
selecting:
   main points
   relevant facts
   key words
inferential reading:
   bias
   opinion
   emotive language
   imagery
   connotations
   proof reading
   comparisons
   style
   tone
   quality
writing for an audience
reporting
summarising
re-drafting
letters
reviews
expressing opinions
structured writing
presenting facts

Media Education
news gathering
editorial selection
representation
audience

Oracy
role play
interviewing
arguing a case
group discussion
planning
evaluation
reporting
telephoning
summarising

**Information
technology**

Design
page layout
fonts
graphics
breaking up text
cartoons

Numeracy
calculating space
distribution charts
costing
keeping accounts

Science
photography
making inks
printing

Business awareness
market research
advertising
banking
selling/distribution
hierarchies
job specifications
accounts

Publishing a newspaper as a
cross curricular activity

Environment
pollution
housing
shops
architecture
landscape
litter
↓

Technology
high tech
innovations
mining
inventions
motoring
↓

**Social
awareness**
old age
leisure
poverty
health
↓

Ad infinitum →

RECORDING AND ASSESSMENT

It is important that throughout the English programme students should be involved in the process of continuous self-assessment, reflecting on how successfully they have fulfilled the aims of the assignments and tasks they have completed. The teacher's expertise in drawing attention to a student's successes and assisting him/her in setting targets for future development, through written comments and discussions, will be informed by detailed knowledge of the attainment targets and the levels achieved. However, it is the dialogue between teacher and student that enables learning to take place and progress to be made, rather than time spent on recording achievements in relation to each separate attainment target on a complex grid.

The proposed system of recording and assessment, therefore, eschews complicated checklists, offering instead a review and assessment sheet to be used, as appropriate, after the completion of an assignment or a number of assignments. The spaces for student comment and teacher comment offer opportunities for summative statements, detailing the progress made in relation to the aims of the assignments which have been completed, thus providing both an extension of the dialogue between teacher and student and a record of the student's achievement. Although the space for the student's comment is placed before that for the teacher's comment, the order in which the comments are completed could vary, depending on whether the teacher wishes to respond to the student's comments.

At the bottom of the sheet are numbered boxes for the teacher to record the student's level of achievement in the attainment targets: speaking and listening, reading and writing. Each attainment target should be assessed holistically rather than by attempting an assessment of individual statements or strands. Experience has shown that, while a sharper focus on the different elements within each attainment target can be extremely useful, there is nothing to be gained by attempting a detailed assessment of each separate statement.

Nevertheless, it is often helpful, when assessing students' levels, to be able to refer to the separate elements within each attainment target. Sheets showing the different elements of the attainment targets for Levels 3–8 are included in the Teacher's Guide.

REVIEW AND ASSESSMENT SHEET

Student's name   Date
_____

Assignment(s) completed

_____

Student's comments

_____

Teacher's comments

ATTAINMENT TARGETS – Levels achieved, ring as appropriate

Speaking and listening		3	4	5	6	7	8	
Reading		3	4	5	6	7	8	
Writing		3	4	5	6	7	8	

NEWSPAPERS: RELATED STATEMENTS OF ATTAINMENT

Reading and responding to newspapers

and

Demonstrating an ability to understand newspaper texts and the techniques used to convey information and opinions in Newspapers.

level

3-8 • to read with understanding an increasing range of non-literary and media texts

---

3 • in talking about texts, to show that they are beginning to use inference, deduction and previous reading experience to find meanings beyond the literal

---

4 • in talking about texts, to show that they are developing their abilities to use inference, deduction and previous reading experience
• to locate information in a variety of texts

---

5 • in talking and writing about texts, to show that they are developing their own views and can support them by referring to some details in the text
• in discussion, to show an awareness of the distinction between fact and opinion in non-literary and media texts
• to use reference books and other information materials to find answers to their own questions

---

6 • in talking and writing about texts, to show that they are developing their own insights and can support them by reference to the text
• in discussion, to identify ways in which the distinction between fact and opinion can be made in non-literary and media texts
• to locate and select information in a range of texts and to use appropriate methods to identify the key points

---

7 • to talk and write about texts giving evidence of personal response and showing an understanding of the author's approach
• in discussion, to show an understanding of some of the features of organisation and presentation that can be used to inform, to regulate, to reassure or to persuade, in non-literary and media texts
• select information from a wide range of reference materials and combine information from different parts of a text or from different texts

---

8 • to talk and write about texts, giving evidence of personal response and showing an understanding of the devices and structures used by the writers, with appropriate reference to details
• write about features of organisation and presentation which are used to inform, regulate, reassure or persuade in non-literary and media texts and show an ability to form a considered opinion e.g. when comparing two texts
• to select and retrieve information from a comprehensive range of reference materials, using techniques such as skim-reading, and to show the ability to evaluate and combine information independently and with discrimination

---

Conveying information and expressing opinions in newspapers

and

Demonstrating the ability to convey information and express opinions in a variety of forms of writing

level

3-7 ● to develop the skills of revising and redrafting their writing

3 ● to produce a range of types of non-chronological writing

4 ● to organise non-chronological writing for different purposes in orderly ways

5 ● to convey information and express opinions in a variety of forms of writing in ways which engage the interest of the reader

6 ● to convey information and express opinions in writing, presenting subject matter to suit the needs of specified audiences and showing the ability to sustain the reader's interest

7 ● to convey information and express opinions in a wider variety of forms (e.g. essays, articles, formal letters) with a clear sense of purpose and awareness of audience, demonstrating an ability to anticipate the reader's response

8 ● to convey information and express opinions in a wide variety of forms with a clear sense of audience and purpose, demonstrating an ability to judge the appropriate length and form for a given task and to sustain the interest of the reader